FATAL ATTRACTIONS

This is the CLEAREST, MOST PRECISE INFORMATION on obsessions, compulsions and addictions. BILL'S STYLE MAKES THE READING EASY while experiencing the pain of seeing yourself on almost every page.

> — Stephen Arterburn
> Bestselling author and founder
> of New Life Treatment Centers

This book is not to increase guilt—but to PROVIDE FORGIVENESS AND VICTORY!

> — Ben Haden
> "Changed Lives" TV-Radio

In *Fatal Attractions,* Bill has dealt with some of the stickier problems common to man. I think you will find his CLEAR, FORTHRIGHT, AND ENGAGING MANNER OF PRESENTATION to be quite helpful, whether you are struggling personally, or helping those who are.

> — Dr. Bill Ritchie, Pastor
> Crossroads Community Church
> Vancouver, Washington

THIS IS A BOOK LONG OVERDUE! Bill Perkins has gotten to the root of all addictions, but in a way that causes the "addict" to sit up and take notice. IT IS A MUST for any who work with people as well as for people with addictions.

> — Bob Moorehead, Pastor
> Overlake Christian Church
> Kirkland, Washington

FATAL ATTRACTIONS

A COMPELLING, HELPFUL BOOK IN SETTING PEOPLE FREE from the bondage of addiction by practical biblical instruction and helpful guidelines. ESSENTIAL READING for the Christian community.

— Dr. Larry McCracken
General Director,
Northwest CBA

BILL PERKINS SPEAKS AS ONE WHO HAS WALKED IN MY SHOES, felt my pain and hopelessness, and now has reached back to help lead me out of my addictive behaviors with COMPASSION AND LOVE.

— Jim McClellan
Host, "The Joy Program," KNMT-TV
Portland, Oregon

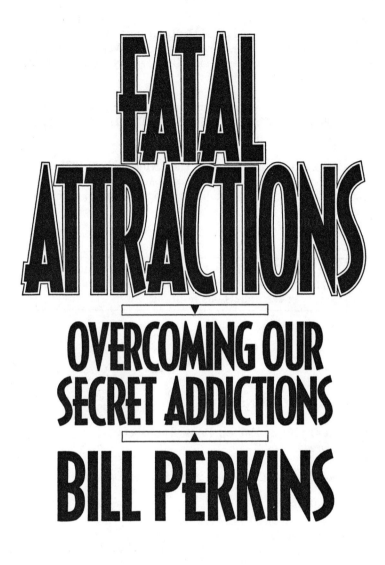

FATAL ATTRACTIONS

OVERCOMING OUR SECRET ADDICTIONS

BILL PERKINS

HARVEST HOUSE PUBLISHERS
Eugene, Oregon 97402

The names and activities of certain persons mentioned in this book have been changed in order to protect the privacy of the individuals involved.

FATAL ATTRACTIONS

Copyright © 1991 by Harvest House Publishers
Eugene, Oregon 97402

Library of Congress Cataloging-in-Publication Data

Perkins, Bill, 1949-
    Fatal attractions / Bill Perkins.
    ISBN 0-89081-921-1
    1. Compulsive behavior—Religious aspects—Christianity.
2. Christian life—1960—   3. Temptation I. Title.
BV4509.5.P47   1991   91-3913
241'.3—dc20   CIP

Printed in the United States of America.

CONTENTS

▼

In Appreciation to ...

My loving wife, Cindy, and my three sons, Ryan, David, and Paul. They always supported me and encouraged my labor.

The wonderful people at South Hills Community Church, who rallied around my efforts and urged me to take the time needed for this work. I'm especially grateful to Dave and Judy Carr, Bruce and Barbara Feil, Bob and Judy Bobosky, Steve and Ila Wilent, Jerry and Melissa Michaels, Bob and MaryAnn Noack, and Mona Krueger.

Eva Gibson, who tirelessly devoted hours to editing the manuscript, and her husband, Bud, who gave up his wife for those hours.

Eileen Mason and the other wonderful people at Harvest House, who had a vision for a book to help people with fatal attractions.

Ed Stewart, who smoothed out some rough spots in the book.

My parents, Lynn and Francis Perkins, who always believed in me.

Eleanor Hunt, whose continual appreciation for my writing stoked my fire.

Rod Cooper, who broadened my understanding of people.

Lance Coffel.

The men who have met with me for years and always speak the truth in love.

All the people whose experiences are mentioned anonymously in this book. I gratefully acknowledge their contributions to my ministry and this book.

I especially thank God for giving me a message of hope.

To the Dragonslayer

Part One

▼

Understanding
Fatal
Attractions

▲

CHAPTER 1

▼

People
with Fatal
Attractions

Y ou might think with the
drought and all Houston
would be hot and dry. It wasn't. It was hot and sticky. It was
the summer of 1979, and it hadn't rained for months. Because
Houston is parked on the Gulf of Mexico, it's always humid—
even during a drought.

The biggest hassle for me that summer was watering my
grass. The city decreed that we could only water between
midnight and six in the morning.

In a way, this book was birthed one Friday night while I
was turning on my sprinkler system. As I walked across my
yard I noticed my neighbors' lights were on. Curious as to
why they were up so late, I approached the fence and looked
through the slats. I expected to see a handful of people playing cards. Instead I saw a young woman talking on the phone.
That wouldn't have been any big deal if she had been dressed.
She wasn't.

I was shocked by my response. Adrenaline rushed through
my body, and I had to pry myself away from the fence.

The next morning I shared my experience with the support group of men I met with weekly. What happened next
gave me a bigger shock than the one I experienced the night

before. Two of the four men confessed that they also had female neighbors they could see through the window at night. Both men had been watching their neighbors for years.

I felt like kicking myself. How could I have been so blind? Since I hadn't struggled with such strong cravings for years, I assumed that my four friends also had their appetites under control. Two of them obviously didn't.

These were mature men with loving families. They were the guys others looked to as role models. But they were hooked and couldn't get free.

A Cry for Help

My mind flashed back to my childhood. Because I grew up in a dysfunctional family, I viewed religious people as different from me. They seemed to have their act together while I was messed up. They enjoyed the straight life and I was wild.

After I graduated from high school, things went from bad to worse. I attended college during the turbulent years of the Vietnam war. Those were times when students wore long hair, sandals, and beads. Confused by a war they didn't want to die in, some of my friends tried to anesthetize their pain with marijuana, LSD, and other mind-altering drugs. And since my life wasn't tethered to anything secure, I also drifted into the drug culture.

I stayed stoned for almost a year. Eventually the emotional pain became too great. In desperation I cried out to God. I didn't ask Him to save me from hell. I needed to be saved from myself and the dragon within who was eating me alive.

My life changed right away. God had been distant. Now He was personal. I soon learned that the grace that had touched my life could help others too. Over time I began to reach out to my friends. During my years at college and seminary I focused my ministry on unchurched high school and college students. Their struggles were similar to those I had faced. I delighted in allowing God to help people through me.

Following my graduation from seminary I pastored a thriving church in Houston. No longer was I a messed-up kid viewing others as normal. I had become normal, as normal as the men in my support group who had just told me about their addictions.

Hooked and Hiding

My friends' revelation made me realize that the church has a serious problem few people talk about. There are men and women—even leaders—who are hooked on sex, food, work, shopping, gambling, exercise, etc. and don't know how to get free. What's more, they're afraid to mention their struggle. They don't want to be rejected. Consequently, many live behind a facade of spirituality to hide what's really happening inside them. Appearing whole and free, they live in the grip of their secret addictions.

As I look back, I'm amazed at how distorted my childhood perceptions were. Good people who attend church and have ordered lives struggle too. Some of them, by the grace of God, have their lives under control. Others have been surprised when they were suddenly unable to control their craving for food, sex, or something else. But, sadly, many people are too afraid to look inside to see what's happening.

Fortunately, my two friends found freedom from their addiction to voyeurism, although it took one of them several years. They're free, but they're still vulnerable. Even today, more than 10 years later, they're susceptible to their former addiction.

One thing's for sure: There are a lot of people like my two friends who need help in overcoming their secret addictions. Perhaps you are among them. On the outside you appear to have it all together. But on the inside things are out of control, and you don't know where to turn for help.

That's why I wrote this book. It grew out of my research, my personal and professional experiences, and my desire to help myself and others understand our secret addictions and experience freedom from them.

The Lens of Truth

My experience with my support group prompted me to read everything I could find on the subject of addictions. I talked with professionals in the field and led support groups of people who struggle with secret addictions.

I don't claim to be an expert in the field of addictions. I've simply tried to gather some of the best, most helpful thoughts on secret addictions. I quote the experts I think have helpful insights, and I point to authorities whose writing provides a more thorough discussion on a particular subject.

I've examined these insights through the lens of truth: the Bible. Why? Because while many experts are providing us with answers, no one's answer is as definite as God's.

I've also included case histories from my experience and the experiences of others. While the names and details have been changed, each story reflects the real-life struggle of someone with a secret addiction.

Because the Spirit of God has the power to transform lives, the insights you will find in this book can liberate you. Not only will you understand yourself better and learn what steps you need to take to find freedom, you'll discover how to tap into God's power for your life.

The Incurable Itch

Once upon a time, a young man moved into a cave in the mountains to study with a wise man. The student wanted to learn everything there was to know. The wise man supplied him with stacks of books. But before he left the cave, the wise man sprinkled a powder on the man's hand which caused him to itch.

Every morning the wise man returned to the cave to monitor his student's progress. "Have you learned everything there is to know yet?" the wise man asked.

And every morning his student's answer was the same: "No, I haven't."

The wise man then sprinkled the itching powder on his student's hand and left.

This scenario was repeated for months. One day the wise man entered the cave, but before he could ask his question the student reached out, grabbed the bag of powder, and tossed it into a fire.

"Congratulations," the wise man said, much to the surprise of the student. "You have graduated. You know everything you need to know."

"How's that?" the student asked.

"You have learned that you don't have to wait until you've learned everything before you can do something positive," he replied. "And you have learned how to take control over your life and stop the itching."[1]

It could be that a secret addiction has created a relentless itch in your soul. You've scratched it hoping it would get better. It hasn't. Instead it demands more attention. You may have told a friend or counselor. But the itching persists, and you can't make it stop.

In a way, that's the aim of this book: to help you take control over your life and stop the itching. Be encouraged. Many people like you have found freedom from their secret addictions. Let me introduce you to a few of them.

Eating Away the Pain

I've seen the grace of God transform a lot of addicts. Sarah is one of them. I'll let her tell her story.

I remember opening the front door of our tiny apartment and setting the groceries on the kitchen table. When I saw that Jack wasn't home I walked into the bedroom and collapsed on the bed. Exhausted, I grabbed a pillow and hugged it. I felt like a child clinging to a teddy bear.

Everything in the apartment was tidy. At least that was one good thing about Jack. He was neat. But honestly, I couldn't think of much else I liked about him.

We had only been married a few months. What a mistake! It made my stomach tighten just to think about Jack. He only cared about himself. I was sick of waiting on him.

Things at work were even worse. My supervisor, the head nurse at a large hospital, couldn't stand me. Instead of praising my cheerful attitude, she told me to wipe the phony smile off my face. Nothing I did pleased her. Nothing! Mondays seemed to be especially hard.

Every day, during my lunch break, I sat at a picnic table in a park, read my Bible, and cried. I felt miserable.

It had been one of those terrible Mondays. I had stopped off at the grocery store on my way home from work to buy bread and milk. I knew Jack loved chocolate chip cookies, so I rounded up the ingredients I would need to make a few batches.

Remembering that the milk was still sitting out, I groaned, sat up, and swung my feet off the edge of the bed. Suddenly I felt a surge of energy. I walked into the kitchen and put the milk and bread away. I wasn't sure when Jack would be home, so I decided to go ahead and bake the cookies for him. He would like that.

As I pulled the first batch out of the oven, I told myself that I would only eat two—no more, just two. After placing the second batch into the oven, I savored my treat. Actually, I was hungrier than I thought.

Since I only had a sandwich for lunch I felt that eating a few more cookies wouldn't hurt.

By the time Jack got home I had eaten all of both batches—except for the five I saved for him. Afterwards I felt ashamed that I couldn't control my appetite and vowed never to let it happen again.

"How was work?" he asked.

"Terrible," I said.

After inhaling all five of his cookies he asked me where the rest of them were.

"I only made one batch," I lied. "I ate a couple and gave a few to the dog," I lied again. "I saved some because I know how much you like them," I explained, not lying.

For the next few days the monster that had been eating at me was silent. Work went smoother, and Jack didn't waste as much time watching television. I seemed to be okay.

On Friday Jack and I had a horrible fight. It was about something stupid. He wanted to go skiing with a friend, but I thought it was a waste of money. Besides, if he was going to ski I wanted to go with him. After he convinced me that the money was no big deal I agreed to let him go. But I was mad. He wanted to ski with his friend because they were both expert skiers. Even though I couldn't keep up with him on the slopes, I still wanted to go.

Jack left early Saturday morning. By the middle of the afternoon I felt like I deserved a treat. After all, he had gone skiing; why shouldn't I do something special for myself? I went to the grocery store and bought a gallon of ice cream and the ingredients for some cookies. This time I spared nothing. I bought tons of nuts and the best chocolate I could find. The monster inside me pleaded for food. I could barely wait to get home and feed him.

This time I had no intention of saving any of the cookies for Jack. He certainly hadn't shared the fun of skiing with me. Once home I locked the door and shut the blinds.

After the cookies were baked I dug in. I ate three batches and most of the ice cream. Finally, the monster was satisfied. But I felt horrible. I wondered where it would end.

For several years I waged a losing battle against a beast of unimaginable power. I went on diets. I joined support groups. I begged God to take away my insatiable appetite. Nothing worked.

I repeatedly vowed never to binge again. But the monster stayed hungry. My enslavement went on for several years. Finally I sought professional help. It took awhile, but over time I began to realize that my compulsive eating was an attempt to satisfy an emotional hunger. I learned that my greatest enemy was an unwillingness to develop an intimate relationship with others, including my husband. Getting my compulsive eating under control demanded that I do something about it. The process of self-discovery was painful. For now, the monster is silent.

Sarah paid the price. She worked hard, and today her eating is under control. Her story has a happy ending.

Desire Out of Control

John, a mild-mannered, personable man in his early 30s, was doing well in business. He spoke with a gentle tone and managed to maintain eye contact with others no matter what was going on around him.

While his wife wasn't strikingly beautiful, she was attractive and supportive. John clearly loved his wife and children and had an effective ministry in his church.

But something was wrong, so John set up an appointment to see me. "I have a problem with pornography," he said. "I do fine for several weeks or maybe even a month. And then I can't resist the urge."

Rather than bringing pornographic videos into his home, John visited adult movie theatres on the other side of town. While he had discussed the problem with his wife, he hadn't been able to find freedom. He had even made himself accountable to his pastor. Nothing had worked.

For a long time he thought his problem would be solved if he moved. In desperation he uprooted his family and moved to another town. He did better for awhile, but then found himself enslaved again. He couldn't understand how something so horrible could have gained such control of his life.

After months of counseling, John learned that he had never identified the behavior that preceded his episodes. It seemed, as with others who have secret addictions, that certain thoughts and activities always led to a pornographic encounter. In the past he had simply tried to stop his wrong behavior. But by the time his preliminary behaviors had progressed several stages, John had gone too far to stop.

One day John realized that dealing with his uncontrolled cravings would involve more than simply saying, "I won't do it anymore." He would have to identify and then stop doing the things that stirred up the cravings. And that's what he did.

Helping Till It Hurts

Cara visited me because of her husband's problem with alcohol. All her attempts to help him had failed. She begged him not to drink. She threatened to leave him if he didn't stop. When he would go out of town on business she would call his hotel to see how he was doing. She felt like he was ruining her life.

After several sessions I asked Cara if it wasn't possible that she needed to stop being so concerned with her husband. I suggested that maybe she should quit trying to force him to do something he wasn't ready to do. Instead, I urged her to look inside herself and see if perhaps she couldn't find some room for growth.

She was immediately defensive and offended by my suggestion that she was a part of the problem. I assured her that her husband needed to control his alcohol use, but explained that she was blaming all of her problems on him. She had allowed her life to center around one thing: rescuing her husband.

Only after Cara was willing to realize that she also had a problem could she begin to release her husband to God and start growing herself.

What exactly was Cara's secret addiction? She was a codependent. Cara had allowed her husband's behavior to affect her in such a way that she was obsessed with controlling his behavior.[2] Cara didn't begin to recover until she realized that, no matter who caused her problem, she had to accept responsibility for herself.

The Dragon Within

There are other stories I could tell. I've seen strong men and women bow beneath the power of an addiction. I've wept with families destroyed by a parent's addiction. I've seen marriages devastated because of a man's sexual addiction or a woman's eating compulsions. I've counseled men and women who have emotionally starved their children because of an addiction to work.

I've related these stories because they illustrate the kinds of struggles people have with their own secret addictions. They also highlight some of the insights that need to be gained for freedom to occur, insights that will be more fully developed as we go along.

Sarah described her secret addiction to food as a monster within her who demanded to be fed. I like to refer to this monster as an evil, powerful dragon. John's inner dragon roared for pornography. Cara's dragon insisted that she control and rescue her husband.

If you're battling a secret addiction, great or small, you know about the dragon within. You wonder how it grew to such dominance in your life. You know if you continue catering to its whims, you'll be destroyed.

But what can you do? You wish you could drive it away. But you can't. Nor can you kill it. The dragon is too powerful.

But that doesn't mean there's no hope or help. The power of your dragon can be broken. There is a Dragonslayer whose strength is available. In this book I'll share many important elements for ridding you of your secret addiction. But ultimately it's the Dragonslayer who will set you free.

▼

CHAPTER 2

Why Do
Bad Things
Look So Good?

I've always been fascinated by things that are off limits. Early in my life I noticed that some of the things I *shouldn't* do often looked better to me than things I *should* do.

I remember being told not to eat candy before dinner. But candy always tasted better than dinner. And hot dogs always tasted better than broccoli.

Once I found a copy of a *Playboy* magazine. I was fascinated by the pictures. My parents told me I wasn't supposed to look at pictures like that. But I thought the undressed women I saw in *Playboy* looked better than fully dressed women.

When I started driving, the law told me always to drive within the posted speed limit. But going fast was more fun than going slow.

I wish I could say that everything has turned around for me as an adult. It hasn't. My doctor recently told me that my cholesterol is in the moderate risk range. As I left his office he handed me a list of foods I'm not supposed to eat. Did the list give me permission to eat ice cream and chocolate cake or roast beef and baked potatoes filled with sour cream? No way! Most of the foods I love to eat are now off limits.

As an avid sports fan, I subscribe to *Sports Illustrated.* Last week I received the annual swim suit issue. Do you think I plucked it out of my mail box, looked at the model on the cover, and said, "What a dog"? Hardly! As beautiful as my wife is, I still find other women appealing.

Forbidden Fruit

Most of us know that chocolate tastes good and that men and women other than our spouses are attractive. Usually it's no big deal. When we encounter something that's expressly forbidden by God or something that's appealing but harmful, we usually resist the urge to indulge.

But occasionally we step over the line. At times everybody eats too much, gazes too long at an attractive man or woman, or drives too fast. That's the nature of humanity. But even when we turn something good into something bad by overdoing it or misusing it, the apostle John assures us that God forgives us and cleanses us when we confess our sins (1 John 1:9).

But sometimes something terrible happens. Sometimes we allow an off-limits activity to sink its hooks into us. Even though we may know that what we're doing is wrong, we do it anyway. We keep experimenting with the tempting object or event, and it makes us feel better. In fact, it makes us feel better *fast*. We like the sudden mood swing, so we want to repeat the feeling the next time we're down.

Over time, our appetites become so strong that we can't seem to resist their call. We find that we aren't just occasionally overeating or gazing at a beautiful man or woman. We're hooked on food, sex, exercise, work, spending, or a host of other things. Our internal appetites are out of control, and we can't shut them off. A powerful, demanding dragon is loose within us.

Bad things look good because they offer us a quick fix to

painful feelings. Like eating candy before dinner, our addictive idols may be harmful. But the pleasure seems too great to turn down.

What Is an Addiction?

But when are we really hooked? At what point does a craving for an off-limits attraction become an addiction? To answer that question we need to understand what an addiction is.

- Dr. Gerald G. May, author of *Addiction and Grace*, defines addiction as "any compulsive, habitual behavior that limits the freedom of human desire. It is caused by the attachment, or nailing, of desire to specific objects."[1]

- In his book, *The Pleasure Addicts*, Lawrence Hatterer wrote that a person can be considered addicted when an "overpowering, repetitive, excessive need exists for some substance, object, feeling, act, milieu, or personal interaction."[2]

- In *The Addictive Personality*, Dr. Craig Nakken states, "Addiction is a pathological love and trust relationship with an object or event."[3]

These definitions, all of which are helpful, come from men who have worked with countless addicts. Some less professional definitions follow.

- "Addiction," said one man, "is an appetite that begs to be fed. It won't stop pleading until I satisfy it. And then, it's only silent for awhile."

- One woman noted, "It's something that's on my mind almost all the time. If I'm awake, I'm either feeling guilty about what I've done, thinking about doing what I shouldn't, or doing it."

- A former addict said, "It's a terrible thing. I know that if I even think about giving in, I'm sunk."

There are almost as many definitions of addiction as there are experiences that represent it. So, you may wonder, which one is right? Actually, they all are. Some describe the cause, some the effects, some the condition, some the symptoms, and some the pain.

I define an addict as *a person who is unable to resist the repeated urge to enter into a love relationship with an object or event for the pleasure and illusion of intimacy it provides.* Addicts find nurturing through the objects or events of their preference.[4] Indeed, their lives have a single aim: the pursuit of the objects or events with which they have developed a love relationship.

- For a sex addict it's pornographic videos or magazines, voyeurism, flirting, illicit affairs, or involvement with prostitutes.

- For the food addict it's certain kinds of foods, such as sweets, or eating in general.

- For the gambler it's betting on a horse or playing the slot machines.

- For the spender it's the excitement of excessively buying clothes, tools, electronic gadgets, etc.

Often our *secret* addictions begin as *hidden* addictions. In the early stages, we aren't even aware that a problem exists. "After all," we argue, "what's wrong with flipping through *Playboy* magazine once in awhile? How can a little playful flirting with the boss be harmful? What's the problem with visiting the refrigerator every half hour for a snack?" Yet sex, food, work, codependency, etc. can be as addictive as drugs or alcohol.[5]

Once we realize, or someone helps us realize, that we can no longer control our cravings, the addiction is no longer hidden to us. We are aware that a problem exists. Yet we tend to keep our addictions a secret. We're embarrassed to admit that something so "harmless" has hooked us. In fact, we may keep it a secret so long that we no longer believe it is an addiction.

Nothing is more important than discovering and dealing with your hidden and secret addictions.

Addicted to an Idol

When we become obsessed with an object or event, it becomes our god. When we give it our time and energy, we are worshiping it. When we depend on it to meet our deepest needs, we're placing faith in it. In short, objects of addiction become idols in our lives.

When we think of idols, the image that usually flashes into our mind is something like the golden calf that the rebellious Israelites danced around (Exodus 32). Since such conduct is rare in the western world, most of us feel we've never practiced idolatry.

But an idol can be any object of extreme devotion, and idolatry is the activity of attaching ourselves to and worshiping that object. The more I understand about addiction, the more I'm convinced it is a deep-seated form of idolatry. The danger we face when we become idolaters is cutting ourselves off from God and others. No wonder idolatry is among those things God expressly forbids (Galatians 5:19-21).

Why would we allow ourselves to enter into a relationship with something harmful? In order to understand how bad things can become so addictive, it's crucial that we understand why bad things look so good in the first place.

In a Garden Long Ago

Whenever I read the account of Adam and Eve in the garden, I can't help but shake my head in amazement. I'd like to think that if I had everything they possessed I'd be immune to temptation. But, of course, I wouldn't be. And neither would you.

Something happened to those two that sheds considerable light on our subject. To begin with, there was nothing inherently wrong with the fruit they were told not to eat (Genesis 2:17). It was something good that God had told Adam and Eve to avoid. It was a test of their willingness to serve God. And its presence in the garden demonstrated Adam and Eve's free will. They didn't have to obey. God gave them the freedom to choose what they would do with their lives.

Sometimes bad things are just good things that are off limits for us. On other occasions bad things are good things used to excess. Certainly there's nothing wrong with sex, food, or work. But they are wrong when used in ways forbidden by God.

That's not to say that some attitudes and actions aren't inherently wrong. Some are. Bitterness, malice, dishonesty, and covetousness are always wrong. So are stealing and slander. But my concern in this book is not with things like these that are obviously bad. We recognize these pretty easily. I'm more concerned about good things that become idols and addictions.

I've often wondered if Adam and Eve would have given much thought to the forbidden fruit if the serpent hadn't spoken with Eve. One thing is for sure: He knew exactly what to say to make something wrong look right.

Like an old friend, the serpent strolled up to Eve and asked, "Did God really say, 'You must not eat from any tree of the garden?'" (Genesis 3:1).

Eve innocently told him that they could eat from any tree in the garden except one. She informed the serpent that if they ate from that tree they would die.

"You will not surely die.... Your eyes will be opened, and you will be like God," he assured her (Genesis 3:4,5).

Suddenly, the fruit on that tree was the most desirable in the garden to Eve. The more she looked at it, the more appealing it became. Satan glamorized the forbidden fruit so that it had a mysterious and magnetic attraction to her.

Even though Eve had everything she needed, Satan deceived her into believing that she had needs God couldn't meet. He tricked her into thinking that, if she would only eat the forbidden fruit, she would become like God.

Did the Devil Make You Do It?

One reason forbidden things look so good to us is because evil spiritual forces in the universe have the power to give them a glitter that attracts. Our dragon gets much of his impetus from the serpent, the devil. They're both out to control and destroy us. The attractions they dangle before us are indeed potentially fatal.

Satan is evil, and he will use any means he can to bring us under his power. When we are devoted to someone or something other than God, we are involved in idolatry and under his dark shadow. The apostle Paul certainly had no misgivings about identifying the spiritual forces behind idols. He warns Christians in 1 Corinthians 10 about the dangers of evil cravings, and declares that people who offer sacrifices to idols are sacrificing to demons (vv. 18-20).

Since Satan has power to glamorize evil objects and activities, making them attractive to the dark side of our personality, we might feel justified in blaming him for our addictions. It's sometimes easy for us to say with comedian Flip Wilson, "De Debil made me do it."

Actually, Wilson's line wasn't new. Adam and Eve tried a

similar approach when God confronted them with their sin. Adam blamed Eve, and Eve blamed the serpent (Genesis 3:12,13). But God didn't buy it. He held Adam and Eve responsible for their actions.

Suffering the Consequences

When I was a child, my dad used to tell me, "Son, if you ever want to drink or smoke, let me know. I'd rather you experiment around me than with your friends."

One day I took him up on his offer. Dad seemed pleased that I had the courage (I later called it stupidity) to ask him to let me smoke a cigarette. He pulled a Camel from his pack and handed it to me. I felt pretty cool as I slipped one end between my lips while he lit the other end.

"Don't just suck the smoke into your mouth," he said. "Take a big puff and pull it into your lungs."

He looked at me with a big smile as I filled my lungs with smoke. Instantly, I felt like someone had placed the nozzle of a flame thrower down my throat and pulled the trigger. I spit out the cigarette and grabbed my chest.

"Pretty good stuff, isn't it?" he asked. He then picked up the cigarette and put it between my teeth. "Go ahead. Finish it."

By the time I had finished smoking that cigarette, I wasn't only sick of cigarettes, I was just plain sick.

I think my dad's actions that day reflect the way God deals with us in our idolatrous addictions. When we turn from God to idols, He doesn't stand in our way. Instead, He hands us over to our lustful cravings. He allows us to become consumed with our passions (Romans 1:18-32). He not only lets us have what we want, He allows us to stuff ourselves with it until we realize how helpless we are without Him.

The misery God sometimes allows us to experience from our addictions is illustrated by an episode of "The Twilight Zone." A restaurant critic dies, but he doesn't know he's dead.

He enters a smoke-filled restaurant and orders his favorite meal. A moment later the waiter places several plates of food on the table. The critic devours the food and begs for more. Never has he tasted such delicious food! He consumes plateful after plateful until the table is stacked high with empty plates.

Even though he's eaten enough food to feed an army, his hunger isn't satisfied. It suddenly dawns on him that, no matter how much he eats, his craving for food is never satisfied. In despair, he cries out. But it's too late. He's in his own personal hell!

Secret addictions can be hell on earth. But God didn't create you for a hellish life. He patiently waits for you to recognize that you are controlled by your appetites and to call on Him to set you free.

Are You Hooked?

It may be that, as you've read this chapter, you've realized that your obsession with something good is really a hidden addiction. But since it's not drugs or alcohol, you don't consider yourself an addict.

Yet your desire to overeat or indulge in pornographic literature seems irresistible. Or you find that you're restless and irritable if you're not working day and night. Or you find yourself shopping and buying things you don't need. Or some other appetite clamors for your attention almost constantly.

Whenever the impulse hits you, you try to resist. Yet the inner discomfort grows. It's like an itch you must scratch. The object or event may not be inherently illegal or immoral, but somehow you know your actions are wrong. You wonder, "How did I get into this mess?"

Addictions don't happen over night. The dragon patiently claws away at our resolve. Innocent cravings subtly take control. In the next chapter we will learn how normal appetites gradually evolve into controlling dragons.

▼

CHAPTER 3

How Do Cravings Get Out of Control?

I can quit anytime I want," Sue insisted.

"Okay, then quit," I said. "I don't think you can do it."

Smiling, Sue picked up her purse and stepped toward the door. "I know I can do it," she said. "You'll see."

While Sue and I met on numerous occasions following that session, it wasn't until months later that she told me what happened immediately after she left my office.

I'll let Sue tell her story.

I hopped behind the wheel of my red BMW and darted away from your office.

It's funny how certain moments in our lives form lasting memories, like riding a bike for the first time or a first kiss. As I look back on what happened that afternoon I vividly remember every detail.

As I headed home I was angry that you suggested I couldn't control my spending. I was already depressed by all my unpaid bills, and I didn't like the idea that I was a shopping addict.

In an instant I decided to settle the issue once and for all. I made a sharp right turn and headed for

Nordstrom's. As I got closer to the mall my heart began to beat faster. Even though I knew I wouldn't buy anything, just the thought of browsing through the store made me feel better.

Once inside, I realized I had forgotten about the semi-annual sale. Everything in the store was marked down. While I knew I wouldn't buy anything, I didn't see any harm in trying on some of the summer dresses.

I found one that was just my color—bright red!

"Sue, you were crazy to tell Bill you wouldn't shop anymore!" I said to myself. "If you were going to stop shopping you should have waited until after the big sale." So I bought the dress, some accessories, and shoes. And I didn't tell anyone.

I tried to rationalize my actions. But in the weeks that followed I realized I had become a slave to spending. I had thousands of dollars in credit card bills. I drove a car I couldn't afford. One day I asked myself, "How did I ever get into this mess?"

Sue's story raises a question that's asked by countless numbers of people every day. People who are addicted to food, sex, gambling, or anything else wonder how it happened to them. Actually, nobody understands exactly what causes people to become addicted. The problem would be easier to untangle if all the stories were the same. But since they aren't, it's hard to identify a single cause of the problem.

But that's not to say we have no idea concerning the process of addiction and how it happens. Indeed, the addictive process follows a well-worn path. By returning to the Garden of Eden we can see the emergence of a pattern. While Adam and Eve weren't addicted to the forbidden fruit, their story illustrates what happens to people in the early stages of an addiction.

Self-Deception

Eve's problem escalated when she convinced herself the forbidden fruit would give her wisdom. Granted, Satan had planted the lie in her mind. But the more Eve thought about it, the more sense the lie made to her. She must have reasoned, "Could something that looks so good really be harmful?" Later she concluded, "If I eat the fruit it will give me life." What a lie!

Once people find themselves losing control, they immediately develop a system of faulty reasoning that justifies their actions. For instance, one of the men I mentioned in the first chapter had been watching a neighbor woman undress for years. As we talked he revealed a sophisticated system of self-deception.

"It's not like I'm a Peeping Tom," he told me. "I don't sneak up to her window and peek in. If she didn't want me to watch her, she would close her blinds."

Amazingly, even in the early stages of addiction, addicts believe their lies. They don't realize they're distorting reality to justify their behavior. From their perspective, their account of what's happening makes perfect sense.[1] My friend convinced himself that his behavior was okay since his neighbor hadn't pulled down her blinds.

Such thinking reminds me of a conversation I had several years ago with my youngest son, Paul. One evening he ran up to me clutching two coins he had found. "Daddy, can I have them?" he pleaded.

"Sure," I answered, "you can keep *one* of them."

Immediately, as I expected, he handed me the dime and kept the nickel. I smiled and explained that the dime was worth more than the nickel. He shook his head in disbelief and insisted that the nickel was worth more because it was bigger.

Paul's reasoning made sense to him. And since he believed he had made the right choice, he had no desire to switch coins. But his reasoning wasn't linked to reality.

In a sense, that's the kind of thinking that characterizes addicts. They redefine reality to justify their behavior. Unfortunately, they believe their distortion of reality is accurate. And since they have deceived themselves, they see no reason to change.

Denial and Blame

It astounds me that when God asked Adam if he had disobeyed, Adam denied being guilty. Instead, he blamed Eve, who in turn pointed a finger of accusation at the serpent (Genesis 3:12,13). It's clear that Adam didn't want to face the truth about what he had done. He hoped to minimize the seriousness of his sin by blaming his wife. Like Adam, addicts deceive themselves by denying the seriousness of their problem and blaming others.

In his book, *Addictive Thinking*, Dr. Abraham Twerski tells the story of an alcoholic who refused to admit that he was the cause of his drinking problems. First, since he only drank beer, he couldn't believe he had a problem. When he began to get sick, he finally admitted that, since he was drinking half a case of beer a day, he was consuming too much fluid. To solve the problem he switched to scotch and soda. When his condition deteriorated further he blamed the soda and switched to whisky and water. When his symptoms got even worse he stopped drinking water.[2]

The denial system of an addict excuses almost any behavior.

- An alcoholic will say, "I'm not an alcoholic. I'm just a social drinker."

- A gambling addict will tell himself, "Golfers spend money on their sport. Why shouldn't I?"

- A sex addict hooked on pornography will say, "It's not like I'm having sex with another person." He may even convince himself that his behavior is strengthening his marriage.

Few people in the early stages of addiction will admit, "I'm hooked and need help." Instead, they deceive themselves into believing their behavior is acceptable.

Rationalization

When we deny something, we refuse to admit it. When we rationalize something, we give good *reasons* for our behavior instead of admitting the one true *reason*.[3] Rationalization enables us to distract ourselves and others from the true nature of our problem.

- Alcoholics may say they drink at night because it helps them fall asleep.

- Shopping addicts may say they spend a fortune on clothes because they need to update their wardrobe.

- Sex addicts might insist they read pornography because their mate doesn't meet their sexual needs.

- Exercise addicts will say they have to run an hour every day and lift weights because they need to stay in shape.

All of these reasons may sound legitimate, but they don't address the real problem.

I recall talking with a woman who managed to break free from a 20-year alcohol addiction. A short time after she quit drinking, she became hooked on pain medication. When I tried to help her realize the seriousness of her problem, she replied, "But, I'm not addicted to these pills. I need them for my pain."

Even though every member of her family knew the woman

suffered from an addiction, she rationalized away her problem. From her perspective, she wasn't addicted; she was merely relieving her pain. As long as she could rationalize her need for those pills she would never have to change her addictive behavior.

Isolation

True intimacy is the greatest enemy of addictive thinking. Since the object of our addiction gives the illusion of intimacy, only true intimacy has the power to burst the bubble of that illusion. Yet as an addiction progresses, we fear telling anyone about it. We're afraid if others know what we have done they will reject us. We're ashamed of ourselves. Besides, we deceive ourselves into thinking we can handle it alone. Instead of reaching out to God and others for help, we withdraw and isolate ourselves.

That's what Adam and Eve did. In order to eat the forbidden fruit, they had to withdraw from God. And after they ate, they tried to cover their wrongdoing without seeking God's help.

Their sin also isolated them from each another. Before eating the forbidden fruit, they enjoyed unrestricted intimacy. When Moses wrote, "The man and his wife were both naked, and they felt no shame" (Genesis 2:25), he wasn't just referring to their bodies. He meant that Adam and Eve were transparent with one another. Since they had done nothing wrong, they had nothing to hide. They had each other and God with nothing in between.

After they ate the fruit everything changed. Their eyes were opened, and they saw their nakedness and covered themselves with aprons (Genesis 3:7). Something had come between Adam and Eve. And something had come between them and God. Afraid of what God would do, they hid (Genesis 3:10).

Nothing characterizes the early stages of addiction more than withdrawal. Slowly, over time, addicts pull away from God and other people. They increasingly turn to the object of their addiction for the illusion of intimacy. As the problem intensifies, their delusional system allows them to justify their isolation. Since they've learned to lie to themselves, lying to others is easy. Gradually they hold onto their idol with both hands, turning their back on the only One who offers them hope for deliverance.

Rituals

In the early stage of addiction, people fight their addictive urges. Instead of giving in to their cravings all at once, they develop rituals which lead to the actual act in small, seemingly innocent steps. Because the rituals appear harmless, the addict can participate in them with little internal resistance. In *Sane Society*, Erich Fromm states that, in a ritual, a person "acts out with his body what he thinks out with his brain."[4]

One man who struggles with an addiction to pornographic movies refuses to read *TV Guide*. When I asked him why, he said, "I don't want to be tempted to watch something that might be bad for me."

Instead, he has developed a "harmless" ritual. He sits in front of his television late at night and plays with his remote control. Rather than *choosing* to watch a sensuous movie from *TV Guide*, he flips from one station to another. Eventually, something erotic catches his eye, and he's hooked. Of course, he never plans on feeding his addiction. Instead, he performs his ritual. The truth is, when addicts decide to perform their ritual, they have also decided to act out their addictive behavior.

A woman with a spending addiction responds to feelings of depression by visiting a shopping mall. She knows that window shopping will lift her spirits. Intending to do nothing but look, she finds herself purchasing items she doesn't need and can't afford. The ritual of browsing through her favorite stores always arouses her addictive cravings that precede her buying binge.

Addicts ritualize the actions they find exciting.[5] Before long they experience exhilaration by just thinking about their ritual. This experience serves a crucial role. It provides a rush and prepares them to act out their addiction.

In later chapters we'll examine the specific kinds of rituals that characterize different addictions and discover how healthy rituals can be developed to replace damaging ones.

Loss of Control

After unsuccessfully fighting their urges for an extended time, addicts try to place limits on their behavior. If they can't beat their addictions, at least they want to control them. When those efforts fail, addicts raise the white flag and surrender their soul to the cravings of the dragon within. Shame is the residue that remains after addicts give in to their addictive cravings.

When addicts finally lose control, major changes begin to occur in their lifestyle.

- The food addict gives in to regular eating binges.

- The sex addict indulges freely in pornography or flirts dangerously with an illicit affair.

- The gambling addict exhausts family resources for the thrill of more action.

- The spending addict runs up huge credit card bills.

By the time addicts have lost control over their life, friends and family members are radically affected by their behavior. Meanwhile, in an effort to diminish the emotional pain, addicts dive more deeply into their delusional system.

Crash and Burn

At some point the physical and emotional stress of addiction begins to break addicts down. All the pain they tried to avoid through their addiction is magnified by the addiction. No longer do the objects or events provide the pleasure they once gave. No longer are the promises of a swift mood change kept. Instead, addicts act out rituals and deeds that almost seem boring.

Life becomes a nightmare. Living in a state of constant anxiety and paranoia, addicts think and do things that frighten them. By this stage in the addictive process, they live on an emotional island occupied only by themselves and their idols. Thoughts of suicide may torment them because it may seem the only sure way of escaping.[6]

Finding Freedom

If you're reading this book for yourself you may be frightened by now. You may have noticed that you're involved in self-deception. You may be believing that your wrong actions are right. You may be justifying your behavior without focusing attention on the fact that you're hooked. You may realize that you're losing control of your life and becoming isolated from those you love.

Or maybe you don't believe you're addicted. If you'd like to find out, simply stop doing what you've always wanted to stop doing. Tell the dragon no once and for all. Stopping for a week or a month isn't long enough. You need to stop today and never start again.

If you can't, you're hooked, whether you admit it or not.

Sue, the woman I mentioned at the beginning of this chapter, didn't realize the seriousness of her problem until she tried to stop. Once she understood she had a spending addiction, Sue took the steps necessary to get her life in order. Although it took her two years to get out of debt, she did it.

Many authorities believe that addictive behavior can't be corrected without outside intervention. Fortunately for Adam and Eve, God didn't passively stand by when they withdrew from Him. Instead, He asked them probing questions, exposed their self-deception, and provided them with everything they needed to move forward with their lives (Genesis 3:21).

The reason healing begins with God is because He already knows the truth about you. He's not blown away by what you've said or done. He sees your flaws and loves you anyway. You're safe with God. True intimacy with Him has the power to shatter the illusion of intimacy created by an addiction. He can break the dragon's power and give you peace.

In the next section of this book you'll gain a clearer understanding of specific kinds of addictions. You'll learn how they're developed and sustained. You'll deepen your understanding of your own struggle and take another step toward freedom.

You may be tempted to turn right to the chapter that deals with the addiction that gives you trouble and skip over the others. Don't do it. There is a helpful overlap in the descriptions of the different addictive behaviors. Reading about all of them will give you clearer insight into those you struggle with and equip you to help other people who are dealing with different addictions. Furthermore, the basic principles for dealing with addictions are applicable to all areas. As you discover how these principles apply in each of the different addictions covered, you will be even better equipped to deal with the dragon in your life.

Part Two

▼

Identifying
Fatal
Attractions

▲

▼

CHAPTER 4

Food—
Hungry for
Love

Nobody is more misunderstood than the person addicted to food. For those not cursed with this affliction, the solution seems obvious. All an overweight person needs to do is stop eating so much. What could be simpler?

Unfortunately, many who are addicted to food also think that's the answer. Consequently, their weight jumps up and down like a yo-yo as they try different diets.

One friend of mine has struggled with her weight for 30 years. She will lose 40–50 pounds during a dieting campaign and look great. Then over several months she'll gain the weight back. After about six discouraging months, she'll go on another diet.

My friend isn't alone in her problem with food. Consider these facts:

- It is estimated that 20–30 percent of the U.S. population is obese.

- As you read these words, 20 percent of all Americans are taking part in a weight-loss program—that's one in five.

- The diet industry generates at least $10 billion per year.

If I was the president of a diet food company, I'd try to shield the American population, especially the female population, from the truth about diets. Why? Because eating addictions can no more be cured with a diet than cancer can be cured with an aspirin.

Eating addictions are deep-rooted problems. Overcoming them requires understanding. I can't utter a few secret words and cause your eating problem to vanish. But I will share some insights to help you identify the cause of your eating addiction so you can start on the road to recovery.

You may remember the antacid commercial which aired on TV several years ago. Staring into the camera was a nauseated-looking man holding his overstuffed stomach. Distraught, he moaned, "I can't believe I ate the who-o-ole thing!"

All of us can identify with that poor fellow, because we've all overeaten. But does occasionally overeating make someone a food addict? Answering that question isn't as simple as saying yes or no. It all depends on why a person overeats.

Compulsive overeaters are people who overeat to satisfy an emotional hunger. They rely on food to anesthetize their emotional pain. They repeatedly enter into a love relationship with food for the immediate pleasure and illusion of intimacy it gives. Food addicts will continue to eat no matter how grave the consequences.

Overcoming Denial

I'm continually intrigued by how hard it is for people, including myself, to admit we have a serious problem. Little struggles, like occasional impatience, are easy to own. Everybody has tiny flaws. But none of us want to admit major distortions in our character like secret addictions.

It's awful to be seen as deficient and undesirable by those we want to like us. Like Adam and Eve after they sinned, we want to hide. We want to shield our weaknesses from others, including God.[1] If we admit we have an addiction of any kind, we will be found out. The deep, dark secret we have tried so hard to hide will be seen. If others see us for what we are, won't they reject us? We think so. Once the dragon in our heart is exposed, we're afraid nobody will desire or enjoy us.

But for compulsive overeaters, the fear of rejection isn't the only reason they deny the seriousness of their problem. Food promises to fill their empty heart without any of the relational risks.

- Food is always there in the crunch.

- Food is always there to kill the pain.

- Food is always there to give pleasure.

No wonder overeaters deny they're addicted. They have a lot to protect. Yet food will never satisfy the hunger in their heart. An empty heart can't be filled until an overeater stops denying the depth of his or her problem.

Keith, a man who visited me for counseling several years ago, was 100 pounds overweight. He came to me because his lack of confidence was hurting him at work and home.

During our first two sessions Keith talked about the abuse he suffered as a child. His mother repeatedly let him know that she preferred his brother over him. Keith had a clear understanding of how that abuse affected his ability to trust in women, even his wife. He also had insight into how his feelings of insignificance undermined his confidence at work.

I finally decided to broach the subject of his weight. "Keith, do you feel your childhood experiences affected your attitude toward food?"

Keith sat up in his chair and crossed his legs. "What are you getting at?" he asked.

"Keith, you're dangerously overweight. Has anybody ever talked with you about it?"

He folded his arms over his chest. "I didn't come here to talk about my weight! I'm a big-boned man. My frame can carry a few extra pounds. Sure, I overeat once in awhile. But if I wanted to lose weight, I'd go on a diet."

"Keith," I said, "based on the conversations we've had, I've concluded you're a compulsive overeater. You've mentioned to me some of your eating binges. I think if you can discover what's driving you to eat like you do, you'll gain some insight into your problems at work and home."

At first, Keith angrily denied being a compulsive overeater. But he didn't stop coming to see me. After several more sessions he began to understand that his deep, inner hunger for love had created an insatiable craving for food. Through a diet he could deny himself the food. But a diet didn't satisfy the hunger of his soul. Admitting the depth of his problem wasn't easy for Keith. But he finally learned that the safety promised by food was an illusion.

Mirror, Mirror on the Wall

Overcoming denial wasn't easy for Keith. It isn't easy for anyone. But it's an essential first step toward overcoming an eating addiction. If you're ready to take an honest look at yourself, the following questions will help you see whether or not you're a compulsive overeater.

- Do you look forward to events primarily because of the food that will be there?

- Do you constantly think about food?

- Do you eat when you're mad?

- Do you eat to comfort yourself during times of crisis and tension?

- Do you eat when you're bored?

- Do you lie to others about how much or when you eat?

- Do you stash away food for yourself?

- Are you ever ashamed about how much and what you eat?

- Are you embarrassed by your physical appearance?

- Are you 20 percent or more over your medically recommended weight?

- Have important people in your life expressed concern about your eating habits?

- Has your weight fluctuated by more than 10 pounds in the last six months?

- Do you sometimes think your eating is out of control?

If you answered yes to several of these questions, you're probably a compulsive overeater.[2]

These questions may reveal to you something about yourself you'd like to ignore. To ignore is to deny. You must face the truth no matter how painful it might be. Once you admit you're a compulsive overeater, you're ready for the next step toward freedom: understanding the addictive cycle.

The Addictive Cycle

Christine dressed like a model on the cover of *Vogue*. She lived with her husband and two children in a beautiful home in an affluent suburb. On Mondays and Tuesdays she worked as a consultant for an advertising firm. She was also active in the women's ministry at her church. Her image was very important to her.

Christine had always been a little overweight, but it wasn't much of a problem. At least that's the way she made it appear. But there was another side to Christine that nobody knew about. Every Monday and Tuesday after work she stopped at the grocery store to shop for her family. In addition to buying groceries, she bought several candy bars and a bag of chips and ate them on her way home.

As a child Christine occasionally ate sweets after a test or an athletic event in which she competed. By the time she was in college she binged after every test. The habit carried into her career. She was ashamed of her behavior, but she felt the food served as a reward for a day of hard work.

To help keep her weight down, Christine often skipped dinner after binging. To purge herself she jogged twice as far as she normally did. Eventually she stopped binging, started a diet, and vowed never again to touch chocolate or chips. But soon she was back to her old habits.

Christine's experience with food illustrates the cycle food addicts are trapped in. Understanding the four steps of the addictive cycle is critical to experiencing freedom from your food addiction.

1. Preoccupation. After Christine starts each new diet, things go well from Wednesday until Sunday—the days she doesn't go to work. But when she's back in the office on Monday, she feels nobody appreciates her contribution. It's just like when she was a kid and her grades were never quite good enough to please her parents.

Back then, food helped her feel better. So by Monday noon, Christine finds herself preoccupied with thoughts of candy and chips. Just thinking about eating makes her feel better. All day she thinks about binging.

2. Ritualization. When she leaves the office she decides to stop at the grocery store. She tells herself she will only pick up a few items for dinner. After all, her family needs to eat.

The ritual of stopping at the store after work seems safe and somehow comforting.

Rituals differ with each addict. Attending parties or banquets can be a ritual that triggers the craving for food in some people. Eating at a restaurant may be a ritual some people use prior to binging. Others may find their hunger aroused by watching TV commercials.

On Monday, Christine's ritual is simply to buy dinner for her family. She avoids buying candy or chips.

3. Acting out. All day Tuesday Christine is obsessed with chocolate. Oddly, her decision to stop binging seems to have increased her appetite. So does grocery shopping. She feels angry because she can't eat what she wants.

Tuesday night she leaves work early. She stops at the grocery store and buys a bag of chips and five large candy bars.

4. Shame. After eating all the candy, Christine's sense of satisfaction is nearly overpowered by shame. "You don't have any self-control," she tells herself. "You really are a bad person. That's why nobody appreciates you. They shouldn't!"

Christine's shame turns to self-hatred, resulting in self-destructive acts. She denies herself nourishing foods for dinner and pushes herself too hard while running.

Other people allow their self-hatred to spew onto family members. Still others eat even more in an effort to put on weight and punish themselves for being such bad persons.

Addictive Thinking

I've chosen to share Christine's story rather than a more dramatic one because it shows a compulsive overeater who isn't seriously overweight. It also demonstrates how food addicts try to feed their empty heart.

Breaking out of the addictive cycle requires understanding the four elements of a compulsive overeater's faulty thinking.

1. I can fill my empty heart by filling my stomach with food. This erroneous thought is the underlying cause of all compulsive overeating.[3]

We all need to feel that we are loved and that our life matters. In healthy families, parents treat their children in a way that communicates they are loved. Children who feel loved view themselves as important. Hopefully, as they grow they will enter into a relationship with God and find their true identity and worth in Him. Loving relationships with parents and with God enable a child to give and receive love from others and prevent an unhealthy craving for love.

When children experience a breakdown in these important relationships, they suffer intense emotional pain. This heartache creates an emotional sinkhole in the heart, resulting in an intensified need for love. Since broken relationships cause the pain, they are reluctant to allow other people to fill the emptiness. Their instincts tell them that vulnerability could lead to further rejection and pain. This is especially true of children who have been abused. Consequently, they are more comfortable with superficial relationships in which they don't have to depend on other people to meet their needs. Yet superficial relationships don't fill their inner emptiness.

Food takes on a special role for people with an emotional hole in the heart. It gives them the illusion of intimacy. Food becomes their lover, friend, and god.

- Food meets any need they have.
- Food nurtures them with taste and texture.
- Food shields them from others with layers of flesh.
- Food punishes them with guilt and shame.

- Food sabotages their marriage or career.
- Food is the weapon they use to rebel.

For a compulsive overeater, food isn't something that merely nourishes the body and sustains life. It's an idol that promises to fill both stomach and soul.

2. I'm a bad, unworthy person. Compulsive overeaters fail to see their value to God or anyone else. We know that we are part of a fallen race. But we are also created in the image of God. As such we are all creatures of eternal value.

Karen told me she could never do anything to please her mother. Every household chore could have been done better. Every grade could have been higher. Every boy she dated could have been sharper. No wonder Karen grew up feeling like a failure.

With tears streaming down her cheeks, she said, "I really believed I was a bad person. As a child I found that food made me feel better for awhile. As an adult I would sneak into my apartment with a gallon of ice cream. But I felt so ashamed after eating it all. I just knew I was the worst person in the world. And then I looked in the mirror. My fat face seemed to say, 'You're a good-for-nothing.'"

As Karen's words emphasize, the agony of self-hatred both drives a person to overeat and is fueled by overeating. When someone experiences the pain of self-hatred and then anesthetizes the pain with food, the result is further self-hatred.

3. No one would love me if they really knew me. This false thought is the natural consequence of the previous one. People who believe they are unworthy don't expect anyone to love them.

Obese people often face rejection in romantic relationships, friendships, and their own families. Statistical research indicates they are less likely to be hired, promoted, or given raises. Why? Because each time an overweight person faces rejection, his belief that he is unlovable is reinforced. The more that belief is supported, the more he is inclined to act unlovable and withdraw into a cocoon of loneliness.

4. *Food is my most important need.* Having cut themselves off from relationships through their faulty belief system, overeaters turn to food as their primary means of intimacy. That's why food addicts are willing to sacrifice their health, family, and friends for the sake of food.

A Better Way

If I make one point in this book, I hope it's that addictions can't be overcome until we admit the dragon has overpowered us and turn to God and others for help. There is neither help nor hope for people who deny the seriousness of their problem.

Denial is dealt a severe blow with the recognition that food only offers the illusion of intimacy. It won't satisfy the hunger in your soul. And a diet alone will only mask the problem. Eventually, what underlies the mask will peek through.

There is a better way. As Karen and I talked one day, she said, "Bill, when I understood that my eating was an attempt to fill a hunger in my heart, a light went on in my mind. Suddenly, I saw how my attitude toward my mother had created that hunger. While I'm not blaming her for my behavior, my response to her criticism created a longing in my soul that I filled with food."

A devoted Christian, Karen had prayed for freedom from her eating addiction. She had memorized Scripture and gone on numerous diets. But nothing brought lasting results until she realized a broken relationship had created an intensified hunger for love that only God and other people could meet.

You may need to evaluate some past pages of your life to see if you can identify the source of your soul hunger. The process may be painful. It often is.

You may need someone beside you as you open the book—someone who loves you, who's not afraid to put his or her arms around you, and who accepts you while not allowing you to deny the truth.

Some people immediately know what caused their hunger. Others require more time to think about it. Perhaps a friend or counselor can help you find the page in your life that tells the story.

Once you've identified the broken relationships or disappointing events that caused your emotional emptiness, you'll find the third section of this book helpful. It's written to aid you in cultivating a relationship that satisfies. It will help you identify the objects of your addiction as well as the rituals you must avoid.

Further Help

For additional insights on food addiction, as well as a thorough discussion of how to identify some of the root causes of compulsive overeating, see *Love Hunger* (Thomas Nelson), by Frank Minirth, Paul Meier, Robert Hemfelt, and Sharon Sneed.

CHAPTER 5

Sex—
An American
Obsession

Several years ago a friend and I were discussing how we dealt with sexual lust. Jim pushed his glasses up on his nose, crossed his arms, and said, "Bill, I don't believe I could ever commit a sexual sin."

Jim must have realized his statement sounded a bit brash. "I mean a really big sin," he explained. "You know, like sleeping with a hooker or having an affair with someone at work."

Knowing he hadn't thought this one through, I asked, "Jim, do you think you're stronger than Samson, godlier than David, or wiser than Solomon? They all had problems with sexual sins."

He shook his head, took off his glasses, and stared at me for a moment. "I see what you mean," he said. "I'd never thought of it like that."

Indeed, nobody is free from the appeal of sexual sins. Even the rich, famous, and powerful are vulnerable. Recently:

• A top-flight NBA player was arrested for soliciting sex from a call girl.

57

- The mayor of a major city admitted having a sexual affair after a videotape showed him with the woman in a hotel.

- A West Coast judge committed suicide when he learned that his sexual exploitation of teenage boys would soon become public.

- A police investigator was arrested for showing his friends child pornography he had acquired during an investigation.

Hardly a week passes without news of a man exposing himself, a woman sexually abusing a child, or a john being arrested for soliciting sex from a police officer posing as a street-walker.

A Big-Time Problem

It would be nice if religious devotion freed us from the threat of sexual addictions. It doesn't. Unfortunately, many churches create an environment where addictions thrive. Addicts crave *secrecy* and *risk*, and the church frequently gives them both.

The excitement of risk is present in a setting where sexual sins are considered the worst of all vices. The greater the wrong, the greater the excitement associated with committing the wrong. Since sexual sins provide such excitement, they carry a strong addictive power. Add to that the church's reluctance to discuss sexual issues and you have an addictive environment.

One authority in the field of addictive behavior told me he believed fundamental Christians and religious leaders suffer from sexual addictions more than almost any other segment of society. Could he be right? Nobody knows for sure. But I do believe more Christians are hooked on sexual sins than most of us would imagine.

I suspect there are countless numbers of sexually addicted people attending church every week who live with the terror of being discovered. When the evening news shows pictures of men being arrested for picking up street-walkers they cringe in fear. A week ago they cruised the same neighborhood.

When the pastor condemns the evils of sexually explicit movies, they nod their heads. Yet the night before they watched a sexually-charged video at home. They're ashamed of their behavior, but they can't stop themselves.

Many women are alarmed, as they should be, at the barrage of sexual stimulation their children are exposed to every day. Yet some of these same woman find themselves enslaved to sexual fantasies. They deal with their consciences by telling themselves they aren't actually cheating on their husbands. Occasionally they try to break free. But the pleasure they derive from their fantasies is so great they can't pull away.

Risking It All

What causes people to continue doing something they know is wrong and has the power to destroy them? It's crucial to realize that a sexual addiction is more than a problem with lust. For sex addicts, the compulsion to act out is so strong they're unable to resist the urge no matter how grave the consequences.

Several years ago a prominent religious leader in the United States was caught in his sexual addiction. He seemed to have it all: a beautiful wife, a charming son, and a ministry that reached millions. Even people who disliked his methods agreed he was a great man.

His world toppled when another minister discovered that this leader frequented the seedy pick-up strip on the outskirts of a major city. Then a prostitute appeared on TV and said the leader invited her to perform a sex act for $10.00.

Confronted by pictures of himself and a prostitute, he reportedly admitted paying the woman to perform pornographic acts. He said he had been fascinated with pornography since childhood.[1]

A He-Man with a She-Weakness

In many ways, this leader's story parallels the story of Samson. Samson was a religious leader who had everything a man could want. But he also had a glaring weakness. He was hooked on sexual experiences that were off limits.

His first recorded words, spoken to his parents, reveal his problem: "I have seen a Philistine woman in Timnah; now get her for me as my wife" (Judges 14:2).

Samson's parents responded to his request with shock and disapproval. They tried to persuade him to reconsider. But Samson refused. His logic was simple: "She looks good to me" (v. 3, NASB).

Like anyone addicted to a sexual craving, Samson withdrew from his family and God. He preferred the illusion of intimacy over the real thing.

Samson's marriage to the Philistine woman was cut short by her death. Afterwards he seemed to have restrained his sexual appetite for 20 years. Somehow he got involved again, and his addiction eventually cost him his life.

The Addictive Cycle

I wish I could travel back in time and talk with him. "Samson," I'd ask, "how did it happen?"

I think he might admit that the addictive cycle led to his downfall. He would probably talk about his mid-life crisis. He had just turned 40 and had done it all. He had crushed the Philistines and ruled Israel for 20 years. Sitting on top of the heap, Samson was bored. Having no goals, he was depressed.

One thing hadn't changed in 20 years: He still liked women. And he probably wondered if they found him attractive.

1. Preoccupation. In his boredom, Samson might have remembered his first sexual adventure in Timnah. Soon he was preoccupied with thoughts of Philistine women. Just thinking about them made him feel better.

He may have eventually decided to travel to Gaza just to look around. It wasn't long before he found himself in the red-light district checking out the women.

2. Ritualization. It's possible that nothing happened on that first visit. But later he made the trip again. This time he may have actually talked with some of the prostitutes. Over the next month the visits to Gaza became a ritual. He walked around town thinking how much fun he could have with a Philistine woman.

Of course, his conscience bothered him. But eventually he learned how to justify his trips. He told himself Jewish women weren't exciting enough. And besides, with a sex drive like his, how could one woman be expected to satisfy him?

3. Acting out. Finally, during one of his trips, he acted out his fantasy. He went to bed with a prostitute (Judges 16:1). For a short time Samson felt alive. The pain of middle-age was numbed. The old exhilaration was back.

4. Shame. Afterwards, Samson felt ashamed. Wanting to keep his actions a secret, he snuck out of her house in the middle of the night (v. 3). Like Adam in the garden, he wanted to hide.

Samson probably vowed to stay away from Gaza. But when the pain of boredom returned, so did his preoccupation with sex. Once again he walked through the town looking at the women. This time his sexual cravings were stronger than before. Again he went to bed with a prostitute and was overwhelmed with shame.

The story of Samson's sexual exploits illustrates the danger of repeating the four-step cycle.

- When repeated, the addictive craving intensifies.
- When repeated, the craving for risk intensifies.
- When repeated, the desire to resist is weakened.

Addictive Thinking

While the addictive cycle explains what addicts go through, it doesn't tell us why they get hooked. Answering that question isn't easy, because different things cause people to become addicted. Yet there are at least four common threads in each story of sexual addiction.

1. I can regularly experience the exhilaration of young love. Many sex addicts are shocked by the excitement they experience the first time they're exposed to the sexual object or event of their choice. While many people might watch a sexually explicit movie and find it arousing, sex addicts experience a major adrenaline rush. The excitement is so great they want to experience it again.

Part of the addiction may be linked to the body's release of adrenaline. As if they had received a direct hit of speed, many sex addicts experience an increase in heart rate, a constriction of the chest, and a warm, pleasurable rush. This reaction takes place in anticipation of acting out. (In Chapters 7 and 8 I will discuss the body's natural release of adrenaline and opiate-like endorphins more thoroughly.)

I can't overstate the importance of this point: Sex addicts aren't only after an orgasm. They want much more. They have entered into a relationship with the object or event of their preference. Their preoccupation with it triggers excitement and anticipation as adrenaline is released into their bodies.

The feelings are similar to those experienced by young lovers. After a date the couple enters the woman's apartment intending just to talk. They say they're not ready for anything more. But each is drawn to the other. In a few minutes they find themselves in a passionate embrace. They're overcome by infatuation and a burning sexual drive.

That moment of sexual excitement and anticipation is what sex addicts are after. They've learned that hunting for the forbidden fruit recreates that feeling. They're aroused by the temptation of breaking the rules.

When the voyeur crouches outside a window hoping for a peek at a woman undressing, he's filled with the same sense of excitement our two young lovers experience. So are the persons hooked on pornography. They have entered into an exhilarating relationship with the images in *Playboy* or sexually-explicit videos. Unfortunately, sex addicts require increasingly distorted and demeaning forms of sexual experiences to maintain the same level of excitement.[2]

2. I'm a bad, unworthy person. This thought pattern is at the core of the addict's self-concept. It's hard to know whether this belief causes or results from an addiction. One thing is certain: After addicts give in to their sexual compulsions long enough, they begin to see themselves as evil.

Men who expose themselves, women who habitually have one-night stands, and other sex addicts don't approve of their behavior. But once they see themselves as rotten to the core, acting out is easier. From their point of view, their evil behavior is perfectly consistent with their evil character.

These feelings of unworthiness are often cultivated by a person's family of origin. Repeatedly in the Old Testament God warned the Israelites that He would visit the sins of fathers upon their children (Exodus 20:5; Numbers 14:18). Nowhere is this more apparent than in the area of addictions.

Many adult sex addicts grew up in families that caused them to associate shame with sex. Men who struggle with visual sexual addictions like X-rated movies or nude dancers often admit they became hooked on pornography while reading pornographic magazines belonging to a father, grandfather, uncle, or other family member.

Often their secret viewings were accompanied by masturbation, which was followed by feelings of shame. Not only does the attraction to pornography carry over into adult life, so does the shame.

Women with sexual addictions frequently have a relative who sexually abused them, either by watching them, touching them, or talking with them in an unhealthy way.

Sexually abused children often feel dirty, ashamed, and afraid they will be abandoned. One of the reasons they fear abandonment is because parents who abused them often threatened to leave if they told their secret. Researchers Eist and Mandel note that, within families where incest has occurred, "Tremendous parental threats of abandonment were a most frequent technique employed by the parent to control or immobilize their children."[3]

Children who fear desertion feel unwanted. It's easy for them to think, "If I'm unwanted, I must be bad."

3. No one would love me if they really knew me. People who feel bad and unworthy because of their sexual addiction avoid intimacy. Instead, they find pleasure in the illusion of intimacy. They feel:

- Real people can't be trusted.

- Real people won't meet their needs.

- Real people bring rejection and pain.

But the object of their sexual addiction always gives them pleasure and an exciting illusion of intimacy.

4. *Sex is my most important need.* This may sound a bit extreme. But at some point addicts become convinced that sexual pleasure will relieve the pain of their unfulfilled emotional needs.

In his book *Intimate Deception,* Roger Hillerstrom observes that, as children, many sex addicts equated love, acceptance, and nurturing with sex. That's why sex addicts are afraid of living without sex. In their thinking, if they don't get it, they won't have love and care. Since they are responsible for getting this need met, they become obsessed with sex.[4]

Sex for Love

Kari, a 25-year-old woman, had such an experience. She told me her dominating alcoholic father used to slip into her bed at night and fondle her. He never made her touch him, and he never attempted to have intercourse with her. "He just touched me," she said.

Even as a small child Kari felt deep shame. But she was afraid to tell anyone. She didn't think her mother would believe her. And she feared a revelation would hurt her dad. Kari felt dirty and believed others would reject her if they knew what was happening.

When she was 14 her father stopped coming into her room. At about that time she discovered other men were attracted to her. Once a man her father's age kissed her. She felt both repelled and aroused. After that Kari found a sense of exhilaration in doing sexual things. She learned to tilt her head, move her mouth, and walk in a manner that captured men's attention.

When she was 15 Kari went to bed with an older man. She felt terrible and excited at the same time. Eventually she was sleeping with a different man almost every night of the week.

Kari feared and distrusted men. Instead of accepting men who initiated a sincere relationship, she chose a free-wheeling sexuality which avoided true intimacy.

Her obsession followed her through college. Attending school during the day and partying at night, she never had any trouble finding a willing partner. On numerous occasions she vowed to change her behavior but couldn't. As her addiction progressed, she became more isolated.

One evening she attended a church single's group with a friend. Hoping to find freedom there, she soon discovered the men at church were also vulnerable to her ploys. Eventually she came to me for counseling.

Kari's story illustrates how compelling a sexual drive can be when people believe that sex is the only way they can nurture themselves. Tragically, the emotional hole is never filled. The more a person tries to satisfy the craving, the worse it gets.

Levels of Addiction

Not everyone who struggles with sexual compulsions is an addict. Some people abuse their sexuality for a period of time and then grow out of it. Many with a regrettable sexual experience in the past put it behind them and move on with their lives.

But as sexual behavior intensifies, sexual addiction escalates. As addicts continue to block the emotional pain, they try increasingly exciting and risky forms of behavior to do the job.

Sex addicts are those whose lives revolve around their addictions. They are losing, or have lost, control of their lives because of their obsessions.

Recognizing how far an addiction has progressed is a crucial step in finding freedom. With each level there are different rituals and cues which trigger the addictive cycle. Understanding these cues and rituals helps people break the cycle.[5]

Preaddiction describes people who begin to find themselves sexually stimulated through impersonal objects or events. Men may be fascinated with pornography and women may indulge in sexual fantasies.

People usually have their lives under control at this level. I've talked with many who contained their compulsions. However, they realize their fascination with sex isn't healthy and could easily become an addiction. They are often troubled by the feeling that the slumbering dragon within could awake and take over at any moment.

For *Level 1* addicts, the dragon has begun to exert his control. This level includes behaviors that society generally considers acceptable or tolerable. These behaviors are seen as "victimless crimes" even though they may exploit others. They include compulsive masturbation, pornography, homosexuality, prostitution, and demeaning heterosexual relationships. Mutual consent between partners may make the behavior at this level seem less addictive.

The single most important aspect of Level 1 addiction is the emergence of the addictive personality.[6] The addictive personality is the part of a person that thrives on the idol of the dragon's preference.

One couple who came to me for counseling expressed frustration about their sexual relationship. The woman felt her husband wasn't interested in her. Later he told me he preferred reading pornography and masturbating. "It's just a lot less hassle." His addictive personality was already well-focused on his sex idols.

Women experience similar struggles. One therapist who specializes in sexual dysfunctions said many of her female clients are hooked on sexual fantasies. "Some women feel their husbands could care less about them," she said. "But their fantasy men look and act in ways that arouse them."

Level 2 addictive behavior involves victims and violations of the law. The activities include exhibitionism, voyeurism, obscene phone calls, and touching a person intimately without consent. Most of the time this person is considered more of a nuisance than a criminal. Yet for the victims the pain is often severe.

Often exhibitionists and voyeurs will carry out their secret sexual behaviors for years. Living double lives, they are in constant fear of being caught.

It's a serious mistake to think that only unsuccessful and unattractive people make up Level 2 addicts. Several years ago one of the NFL's leading pass receivers was arrested for exposing himself to young girls while he sat in his car.

Level 3 addiction involves serious crimes in which severe damage is done to the victim. Rape, incest, and child molesting are at this level.

How to Know If You're Hooked

Patrick Carnes suggests a four-step formula aimed at helping people discover if they have a sexual addiction.[7] While asking yourself these four questions, it's crucial that you are brutally honest. Remember: You can't deal with the dragon if you deny that he exists.

1. Is your behavior a secret? Are you doing things you refuse to tell others about? Do you feel if those closest to you knew what you were doing they would reject you or strongly disapprove of you? Are you telling lies to camouflage or disguise your behavior? If so, you're probably plagued with shame and living a double life.

2. Is your behavior abusive? Does your sexual behavior create pain for yourself or others? Is it degrading or exploitative of others? If so, it could be the kind of behavior that will stimulate an addiction.

3. Is your behavior used to deaden painful feelings? Are your sexual actions an effort to change your mood rather than express affection? Anytime sexual behavior is used to erase pain, it's part of an addictive process.

4. Is your behavior empty of genuine commitment and caring? Are you substituting the illusion of intimacy provided by an object or event for the genuine intimacy of a healthy relationship?

The Moment of Truth

Answering these questions honestly will alert you to the presence of addictive tendencies. Unfortunately, most addicts avoid honesty as long as possible. Eventually, however, the moment of truth will arrive. Something will happen to force them to admit their life is out of control because of their sexual addiction. Consider the following scenarios.

- You come home from work and a police car is waiting at the curb. Your neighbor has identified you as a Peeping Tom.
- The school counselor phones. You've been reported to the child care agency for sexually abusing your child.
- Your children discover the X-rated videos you had hidden.
- Your spouse leaves you after finding out you had another affair.

For Samson the moment of truth arrived near the end of his life. Blinded by lust, he slept in Delilah's lap while she cut his hair. A moment after the last strand fell, the Philistines arrived.

Samson had been caught and didn't even know it. Immediately he leaped to his feet as he had done before, expecting to fight off his enemies. But stripped of his strength and isolated from God, he was powerless to resist.

Samson had fallen. He would never gaze at another Philistine woman. They made sure of that when they gouged out his eyes (Judges 16:20,21).

Many people believe Samson's story ends on a tragic note. I don't. Blind and imprisoned, his hair began to grow and so did his relationship with God. The Lord forgave Samson and used him one last time. The hero of Judah pulled down a Philistine temple, destroying his enemies.

Samson learned firsthand what all addicts need to know. God is the God of the first and second and third and fourth chance. He never gives up on us.

I hope you won't wait for a moment of truth to force you to admit your problem. If you're hooked at some level, the third section of this book is for you. It will help you understand yourself better and give you some specific suggestions to help you cooperate with the Dragonslayer to secure your freedom.

Further Help

For literature and information regarding support groups in your area, write the headquarters for Sexaholics Anonymous: P.O. Box 300, Simi Valley, CA 93062.

For additional insights, the following books will be helpful:

Joe Dallas, *Desires in Conflict* (Harvest House Publishers).

Patrick Carnes, *Out of the Shadows* (CompCare Publications).

Grateful members, *The Twelve Steps for Everyone* (CompCare Publications).

▼

CHAPTER 6

Codependency— Hooked on Helping

If I'd known 15 years ago what I now know about codependency, it would have saved me a ton of heartache. But I didn't. I now realize that codependency may be the most common family problem. It happens to everyone who lives in a dysfunctional family, that is, a family that doesn't fulfill its God-intended function.

While a variety of definitions of codependency exist, I like Melody Beattie's. She says that codependents are people who let another person's behavior affect them and who are obsessed with controlling that person's behavior.[1] Codependents become so focused on rescuing others that they ignore what's happening inside themselves.

A Family Album

How does a person become a codependent? As children grow they learn unwritten rules for relating to other people. Children raised in dysfunctional families learn to react to the primary stressor in the family. This could be a parent's alcohol or work addiction, physical or verbal abuse, emotional control of everyone's feelings, religious rigidity, or sexual abuse.[2]

Before the addiction, the family is in balance. Once the shift takes place, each member finds the imbalance intolerable. They individually adapt to the stress in an attempt to control it and bring balance. As long as the stress exists, family members live in a constant state of readiness to cope with the stress. Over time, each one assumes a codependent role in the family.

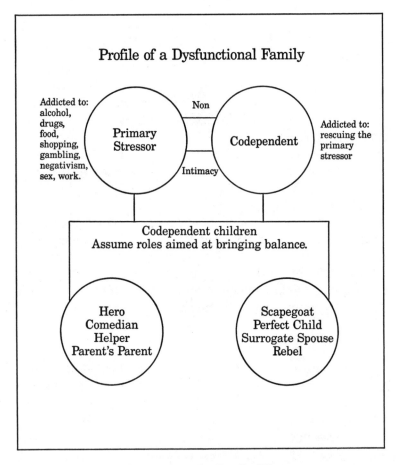

A Picture from the Family Album

For instance, in a stress-filled family, one child may assume the role of the *family hero*. This child is out to save the family name. He is usually driven to excel in everything he does. As adults, family heroes often become workaholics in helping fields such as medicine, social work, or church work.

Another child will take on the role of the *comedian* to provide comic relief for the family. The comedian diverts attention from the real issues by clowning around and attracting attention to himself.

One child may become the family *scapegoat*. He detracts attention from the problem with inappropriate and sometimes antisocial behavior. The scapegoat needs attention and gets it with his bad behavior.

The *perfect child* in the family is the forgotten child. Nobody has to worry about him. He expresses no needs and is rewarded for it.

Other roles children may assume in dysfunctional families include the *helper*, the *surrogate spouse*, and the *parent's parent*.

When the children of dysfunctional families grow up, they continue playing their roles even though they are no longer connected to the original sources of their stress. Their roles still seem normal to them since they grew up with them. But even though these roles were helpful at one time, they eventually become destructive.[3]

Hero at Large

While growing up I became the family hero. I had to be tough and competitive. I had to let go of my feelings of compassion, fear, and vulnerability. Obviously I wasn't aware of my codependency. I certainly didn't think I had a problem. On the contrary, I viewed myself as a highly competitive and competent person.

I could tell numerous stories about people I've tried to rescue. Don't misunderstand me. I'm not talking about offering guidance to people in need or assisting people who ask for help. I'm talking about being driven to rescue people I thought had great potential. I'm talking about assuming responsibility for the success of people I didn't think could make it without me, people like Kent.

One afternoon, Kent, who looked like the cowboy in the Marlboro commercial, dropped by my office. "I'm building a first-class athletic club in downtown Portland," he drawled. "I'm revamping an old building. It's going to be nice—*real* nice."

"How long have you lived in Portland?" I asked.

"I moved here several months ago from New Mexico. I had several clubs there. Before that I owned clubs in Arizona and Colorado."

"How did you get into the athletic club business?"

Kent sat up in his chair. He flashed a broad smile. "I used to be a professional kick boxer. Twice I fought for the light heavyweight championship of the United States. I got into the business while training as a fighter. Later I wanted to get into movies, but it didn't work out. I got strung out on alcohol and drugs. A few years ago I came to the Lord. It's really made a difference."

The more Kent talked, the more I liked him. Kent was dynamic and influential. I saw tremendous potential in him.

For almost a year, I tried to get together with Kent every week. He said he wanted my help, and so I gave it to him. He wasn't very reliable about keeping appointments, but I continued to meet with him. Even though he indicated no willingness to change, I didn't give up on him. I imagined what he would be like when he got his act together. I intended to be the person to help him find out what he could become.

One morning Kent failed to show up for a breakfast appointment. It wasn't the first time. But on this occasion, he sent his business partner. That was the day I learned why Kent had shattered two marriages, run through several successful businesses in three states, and occasionally stood me up.

Kent was strung out on coke. He had been for years.

Amazingly, he had surrounded himself with people who covered for him, put up with his lack of consideration, kept him from being responsible for himself, and added dignity to his lifestyle.

As I left that breakfast appointment I felt used. I was ticked at Kent. He obviously didn't appreciate the sacrifices I had made for him. Nor had he taken my advice.

How did I respond? I withdrew. I persecuted him by cutting him off emotionally. Kent retaliated by accusing me of not being there when he needed me. Suddenly, I had become the victim.

Who's the Victim Anyway?

I've told this story because it illustrates how my childhood role as the family hero carried over into my adult life. I wanted to help Kent more than he wanted to be helped. It also shows how, over time, a codependent can become both the persecutor and victim.

Stephen B. Karpman compares the roles a codependent plays to the three points of a triangle. First, we rescue people. Second, when they don't respond the way we want them to, we get mad and persecute them. Finally, we feel used and end up being punished by the person we tried to rescue. We become the victim.[4] I carried out all three roles with Kent and with others.

Until I began to understand codependency I never knew why I was attracted to troubled people with great potential. I didn't understood why I continued trying to rescue them after they dumped on me. Too often my motive wasn't to honor God. The payoff for me was the emotional pleasure I derived from rescuing someone. I liked the thought of being someone's hero. It made me feel good.

Codependency in the Church

I'm convinced that the church nurtures codependent relationships. At times we even inadvertently train people to be codependents. We teach, as we should, that self-sacrifice is the highest form of love. The problem is people learn how to act lovingly and sacrificially without being loving. Codependents are really helping themselves. They enjoy the feeling of power they have during the rescue. They feel righteous and good about helping others. Unfortunately, such rescuing is a subtle form of self-glorification.

And what happens when the persons being rescued don't respond as expected? Codependents become angry. They feel they've been taken advantage of. They persecute and then become the victims.

It's easy to forget that rescuing people is God's job. We're simply to share His love. We're there to help people who are willing to be responsible for themselves.

My attempts at rescuing people who weren't ready to be rescued never helped anybody. On the contrary, it actually slowed their growth by protecting them from the consequences of their actions. Most people refuse to change until they experience the painful consequences of their bad choices. God never relieves people of their responsibilities or the consequences of their actions. And neither should we.

Destructive Actions

Behavior that helped us survive as children doesn't go away easily. Even though the original cause of our behavior is gone, we tend to continue acting in the same way. After all, it worked in the past. Unfortunately, some codependent behaviors, like the following, can be harmful.

Reacting. When we react we are immediately and thoughtlessly pulling in the opposite direction from another person.

We feel things are out of balance, and we react to get them in balance.

When Jesus visited the home of Martha and Mary, He walked into a brewing conflict. Martha had worked hard to make the Lord's visit special. She had prepared a delicious meal. When Martha didn't feel Mary was carrying her end of the load, she reacted. Martha chided her sister and rebuked the Lord for not caring (Luke 10:38-42).

Adults who grew up in a family that went from one crisis to another learn to react. Sometimes we react because we're embarrassed by the behavior of another person. We want to fix the damage their behavior has caused. We want to shield them and ourselves from what's happened.

Controlling. Codependents also try to control others.

Kip's husband had a drinking and sex addiction. Every couple of weeks he would drink too much, visit nude bars, and watch pornographic movies. Kip did all kinds of things to try and control his addictions. She supervised him, went out in the evenings and searched for him, called all over town, forced him to go to a counselor, searched his clothes for clues, and yelled at him.

Kip did it all in the name of love. She said she was only trying to help. On the outside she appeared sweet and caring. She said she just wanted her husband to obey God.

On the inside Kip was desperately trying to force her husband to bow to her will. She felt it was her job, not God's, to fix him. She refused to let go of the reins and allow the man's life to follow its natural course. She refused to move aside and allow God to make him so miserable he wanted to change.

Did Kip's controlling behavior do any good? Of course not! It never does! Instead of controlling her husband, she was actually placing herself under his control.

After some extensive reading and painful counseling, Kip released her husband to God. Slowly he began to change.

Even if he had never changed, Kip needed to let go. Otherwise her husband would continue to resist her control. He would repeatedly punish her for making him do things he didn't want to do.

Rescuing. What prompts us to keep trying to rescue people who in turn make us their victims? As with other addictions, a poor sense of identity drives much of our behavior. Children who grow up in dysfunctional families often fear abandonment. They don't receive the affirmation and nurturing needed to make them feel safe and secure. Consequently they believe something is wrong with them.

In order to feel worthwhile, they'll do anything. Early on they learn that taking care of others in the family makes them indispensable. It makes them valuable. Codependency drives people to find their identity in other people instead of in God.

Negative Emotions

The next time you find yourself trying to rescue someone, watch for a shift in your mood. If the person you're trying to help doesn't respond the way you want, or if he fails to express appreciation and you feel used, your motives for helping him may have been self-serving. You were likely trying to rescue him so you would feel better about yourself rather than because you genuinely cared for him.

The following emotions may alert you to your codependent tendencies.

Disappointment. Perhaps the greatest emotional pain a codependent experiences is the pain of disappointment. The life you hoped for and worked for may never materialize. The person you slaved to help may turn against you.

I understand such disappointment. Years ago a young man, Sean, joined the staff at the church were I was the senior pastor. Seldom have I clicked so quickly with another person. He was the brother I never had. The two of us dreamed about a lifetime of ministry together. In a short time he had built a thriving youth ministry in our church.

As our friendship grew, Sean became more abrasive with me. I told myself he was immature and just needed more time. After all, nobody's perfect. I wasn't worried because, as a hero, I knew I could help him.

Occasionally friends pointed out to me that Sean's problems were more severe than I thought. People who had known him in his previous ministry warned me about him. When I talked with him about what I had heard, he said these people were lying.

It was easy for me to trust Sean. I had learned as a child to see the best in people, especially people with serious problems.

Late one night I received a phone call from another pastor informing me that Sean was sexually involved with a single girl. Heartbroken, I confronted my friend. Rather than accepting my help, he turned against me. The rescuer became the victim again.

Others have seen their dreams of a loving marriage shattered by an alcoholic spouse who refused all help. Parents have suffered the disappointment of a child hooked on drugs who rejects them and everything they have to give.

Certainly, we should grieve over our losses. It would be unloving and inhuman not to suffer pain after such disappointments. But a codependent has a way of searching out relationships that will end in disappointment. We keep going back for more punishment.

Guilt. One reason we persist in our efforts to help other people is because we feel responsible for their failures. Since we're trying to rescue them, we blame ourselves when they don't get better. We feel guilty.

Obviously, there are times we should feel guilty. If we've

done something wrong, our conscience should tell us. When it does we need to confess our sin to God and accept His forgiveness and cleansing (1 John 1:9).

On other occasions we experience false guilt, that is, we feel we've done something wrong when we haven't. Inappropriate guilt occurs when something happens that's beyond our control.

When a child tries to save a parent's marriage and it ends in divorce, the child may feel responsible. He isn't. After Sean became sexually involved with a single woman, I felt responsible. I wasn't.

Unresolved guilt can result in self-hatred which drives the codependent to try harder to help someone who doesn't want to be rescued.

Anger. When disappointment and guilt aren't properly dealt with, they can lead to anger. I'm not talking about justifiable anger. When we see an injustice, we *should* feel angry. It may drive us to do something to right the wrong.

The kind of anger codependents often experience results from years of disappointment and guilt. It's an unhealthy anger that occurs because an expectation hasn't been met. They feel they've lost something of value.

When this kind of anger is suppressed, it causes ongoing feelings of rage. Periodically, this anger will explode. I've witnessed violent and frightening outbursts of anger when an addict refuses to bow to the demands of a codependent.

Some codependents are too controlled to have a violent outburst. Instead their anger seeps out like acid. They use sarcasm to bite away at the person who has resisted their rescuing attempts.

Finding a Way Out

Working through codependent behavior requires both understanding and effort. Spend time thinking about the role you had in your family while growing up. Look at your present relationships and see how you still function in that role.

Don't search through the pages of your past looking for someone else to blame for your present problems. Instead, try to understand why you are the way you are so you can more easily change.

As you begin to uncover your codependent tendencies, there are two specific steps you can take to start dealing with them.

Let go. One thing that makes overcoming codependent behavior so hard is feeling the need to hold on and control people in order for them to recover. Holding on seems like the safe thing to do.

Such isn't the case. Nobody will ever get better because you forced them to. You can't rescue people who aren't ready to be rescued. The best thing you can do for them is let them go and trust God to take care of them.

Consider the story of the prodigal son (Luke 15:11-32). When the son demanded his inheritance, his father gave it to him. When the son wanted to leave, his father let him go. After he departed for the distant country, his father didn't search for him.

Eventually, when the boy ended up in a pig pen, he came to his senses and returned to his father. When he returned, his father rejoiced.

What would have happened if the father had followed his son to the distant land? He would have seen him wasting his money on wine, women, and the wild life. Maybe the father would have stepped in and tried to reform him.

Would his intervention have helped his son? Of course not! The boy needed to reach a place of desperation. Few addicts are willing to stop their destructive behavior until the pain of continuing is greater than the pain of stopping. By letting go of his son, the father actually speeded up his recovery.

If you've focused your life on trying to rescue others, you need to let go of them. Continue to love them, but stop trying to control their behavior. Trust God to work in their lives.

Letting go doesn't mean you approve of wrong actions. Nor does it mean you never confront wrong behavior. And it certainly doesn't mean you don't care. Instead, you stop allowing yourself to be obsessed with rescuing people by controlling their lives.

You can show compassion and concern for friends and family members without rescuing them. When people share their problems with you, ask, "What do you need from me?" Once they've told you, decide whether or not you're able to help them. Set a limit on what you can do. If the timing isn't right for you to help them, say, "I can't help you." Or it may be appropriate for you to simply listen and tell them you're sorry they're having problems. Offer your prayers and leave it at that.

Find the new you. Since your codependent behavior is rooted in your family of origin, part of the healing process involves recognizing that you don't need to function in those learned roles any longer.

I don't need to be a hero for my family or church. God didn't call me to rescue people who aren't ready to change. And God didn't call you to rescue your parents, spouse, children, coworkers, or friends. In fact, as I understand the Bible, He didn't call us to rescue anyone. God does the rescuing. We are called to obey Him and trust Him to touch lives.

Overcoming codependent behavior involves more than understanding how our present behavior developed. Our inaccurate sense of identity is what drives us to rescue people. We feel safe and secure when we're needed. We feel righteous when we think we're helping deliver someone from their mess.

We need a new sense of identity that gives us security. We need to know how to think when we find ourselves tempted to rescue someone who doesn't want our help. In the final section of this book, you'll gain some insights that will help you find the new you. You'll learn how you can be healed from your addiction to codependency.

Further Help

For additional insights, as well as a thorough discussion of codependency and how to overcome it, the following books will be helpful.

Pia Melody, *Facing Codependence* (Harper and Row).

Pia Melody and Andrea Wells Miller, *Breaking Free: A Recovery Workbook for Facing Codependence* (Harper and Row).

Robert Hemfelt, Frank Minirth, Paul Meier, *Love Is a Choice* (Thomas Nelson Publishers).

John Bradshaw, *Bradshaw on the Family* (Health Communications, Inc.).

Melody Beattie, *Codependent No More* (Harper and Row).

▼

CHAPTER 7

Exercise— The Natural High

I've always loved those "lazy, hazy, crazy days of summer." When the days start getting longer and hotter, my thoughts drift back to my high school years.

Even though summers in Austin, Texas, were sizzling hot, I thrived on the weather. Five or six mornings each week John Ballard and I would climb into my dad's '56 Pontiac and wind our way over and around the hills of central Texas. Our destination? A boat dock on the shore of Lake Austin. We could see glassy smooth water stretched out for miles. We lived to water ski.

My love for sports continues to the present. Whenever I meet or read about sports fanatics, I tap into their enthusiasm. That's why I think I'd like Dan Marineau. He's a compulsive surfer who gets up early in the morning to look for waves.

"I'm addicted to surfing," he says. "It's more than a passion; it's the greatest natural high I've ever experienced. I've never had anything I've enjoyed so much. Surfing made me travel, and it makes me want to travel more."

Only 21 years old, Marineau has surfed around the Pacific Ocean, chasing waves from Hawaii to New Zealand. He's lived in a VW bus on the south jetty in Florence, Oregon, to take maximum advantage of winter waves. Surfing is his life. He says, "I have to be able to see the ocean and see what the surf is like. I have to surf every day or I'll be grouchy."[1]

The Opiate of Exercise

Like Marineau, many people are hooked on some kind of exercise: running, aerobics, skiing, or one of a host of other physically demanding activities. The thrill of competition and pleasure of exercise is an addiction. They get high on one of two kinds of natural drugs produced and released by the body during physical exertion: adrenaline and endorphins.

Adrenaline. Dr. Archibald D. Hart notes, "One of the commonest ways we pursue this goal of exalted delight is through the use of the body's own natural and powerful stimulant—adrenaline."[2] Adrenaline helps us cope with emergency situations by preparing our bodies to run or fight. It gives us extra energy, strength, and alertness. Over time a person can become hooked on the pleasurable feelings produced by adrenaline.

An adrenaline rush is experienced by risk-takers, people who like exciting, pressure-packed situations. Sky divers, skiers, and bungie cord jumpers are among those who seek high-risk activities and the natural high they produce. Those who compete in high-risk or fast-paced sports such as surfing or sky diving are probably driven by the need for excitement. Without their sport they think life's a drag.

Unfortunately, when people develop a lifestyle that continually taps into their adrenaline supply, their bodies function in a constant state of emergency. Because adrenaline produces a rush of pleasure like speed, some people seek out situations that infuse them with this potent stimulant.

As with any drug, the body will eventually adapt to the high level of arousal adrenaline produces, so the addict needs more of it to achieve the desired effect.[3] Like Daniel Marineau, who gets grouchy when he can't surf, they experience symptoms of withdrawal.

Endorphins. Other forms of exercise offer a different variety of chemical pleasure. Distance runners, aerobics practitioners, and others who sustain exercise over an extended period of time often experience another kind of rush. For example, distance runners experience what is called the runner's high, a feeling of power, dissociation from the body, and lightening of the physical being. Unlike the adrenaline rush of the thrill-seeker, the runner's high is almost a trancelike state. The runner feels happy and content and seems to float above his running body.

For years scientists wondered why running or extended aerobic exercise created such a pleasurable feeling. During the mid-1970s the substance that accounted for the runner's high was isolated. Researchers discovered that the body manufactures opiate-like substances, called endorphins, that are picked up by the receptors on nerve endings, many of them near or in the brain. These opiates alleviate pain and discomfort while also elevating the mood. The high not only happens during the activity but for several hours afterward. The release of endorphins is stimulated by numerous things, including strenuous physical activity.[4]

When exercise addicts stop working out they cut off their supply of endorphins. As with those denied adrenaline, addicts deprived of endorphins experience withdrawal symptoms such as depression and overall mood disturbances.[5]

Overdoing a Good Thing

It's not hard to figure out why so many Americans have given up the easy chair and footstool for the running track or gym. Certainly the physical and psychological benefits of exercise have been a driving motivation. People who exercise regularly enjoy better cardiovascular health, improved muscle tone, lower body fat, lower blood pressure, lower cholesterol, and better sleep. Psychologically, they feel better about themselves. Not only do they enjoy the pleasure of being in shape, they also bask in the compliments of friends who notice how much better they look.

With so many positive benefits of physical exercise, you may wonder how it can become such a demanding dragon for some people. For exercise addicts, working out is more than something they do to stay in shape. *They have entered into a relationship with an experience that temporarily deadens their emotional pain and provides them with pleasure.* In order to perpetuate these perceived benefits they will exercise harder and longer or seek more exciting experiences. Ironically, their craving for exercise often threatens their health and disrupts their relationships with family and friends. Yet when deprived of exercise they feel down. The thought of cutting back seems absurd.

Connie Chan, clinical psychologist and assistant professor of human services at the University of Massachusetts at Boston, states that the typical exercise addict is a female or male between the ages of 20 and 60. These people began exercising as a way to lose weight and become more physically fit.[6]

But once they pay the price for getting in shape, exercise addicts push themselves thinking the benefits will increase. When they look in a mirror they're spurred on to work harder. Every time they attend an aerobics class, pump iron, swim, or bicycle they are drugged by the experience and gratified with the benefits. They want more. They convince themselves that the more they exercise the better they'll feel.

Richard Benyo, former executive editor of *Runner's World* and author of *The Exercise Fix*, tells the story of a California runner, Joe Oakes. When Joe was 40 he weighed over 200 pounds. He began exercising in an effort to get his weight under control.

But the more Joe ran, the more he enjoyed it. At first he

only ran quarter-miles. Over time he worked up to running five miles at a time. Later he ran marathons and then ultra-marathons. Each time he ran a greater distance he wanted to try something more.

Hoping to satisfy his craving for more, he ran in the Western States 100-Mile Endurance Run, finishing in under 24 hours. Then he decided to try triathalons, consisting of long-distance swimming, biking, and running. Six times he competed in the Iron Man Triathalon in Hawaii. Once he competed only eight days after breaking three ribs, a shoulder, and a wrist when a car hit him while he was training on his bicycle.[7]

After that painful race in Hawaii, Joe finally realized he was hooked on exercise and took steps to get his life under control.

When Is Enough Too Much?

Perhaps you go for high-risk activities that give you an adrenaline rush. Or maybe you're a runner or aerobic practitioner who thrives on the pleasant sensation of endorphin stimulation. In either case, you need to evaluate your exercise routine to see if you're dangerously hooked. If you are, beware. Your health and the well-being of your relationships are at risk.

The following questions will help you determine whether or not you're becoming or have become an exercise addict.

- Do you exercise through pain rather than cut back and wait for your body to heal?

- Do you find yourself exercising harder and harder in order to achieve the same pleasurable effects?

- Do you experience depression, moodiness, and irritability when, because of injury or schedule conflicts, you stop your activity?

- Do you find yourself looking for bigger challenges and greater risks in order to achieve the same rush you experienced when you first started your activity?

- Do you find your mood altered during the course of your regular aerobic program?

- Have friends or family members expressed concern about the time you spend competing or working out?

- Have members of your family told you they think your sport or exercise routine is more important to you than they are?

If you answered yes to one or more of these questions, you're either hooked on exercise or on your way.

Driven to Feel Good

Because people who exercise religiously are usually in top shape, it would be easy to assume they like themselves. That's not always true. While they may enjoy the benefits of good conditioning, they often wish they were more competitive in their sport. Others wish they were in even better shape.

We all have shameful secrets about our families and ourselves, dark memories we would like to hide from others. We fear if others see us as we really are they will reject us. Few things can deaden the pain of the shame that attacks our pride more effectively than exercise. It burns away unwanted fat while toning muscles, giving us something to feel good about.

But exercise addicts turn a good thing into a bad thing by going to extremes. Kylie is an example.

Kylie struggled with her weight throughout high school and college. Following graduation from college she landed a good job in a growing company. One of the benefits of her job was a membership at a nearby athletic club.

After attending aerobics classes for several months, Kylie liked how she felt and looked. Soon she was obsessed. She tried to attend an aerobics class every day and get into the weight room every other day.

Kylie learned to exercise through her pain. But she wanted more. She started training for marathons. At times she ran for an hour after her aerobics class. "I've always been a driven person," she explained. "Once I plugged into an exercise routine, I gave it all I had."

One day she woke up and could barely walk. She went to her doctor, and he told her she had injured her knee and needed to rest it for several weeks. During her time off, Kylie realized she was addicted to her exercise routine. She had allowed it to replace her work addiction.

What was behind Kylie's compulsion to overexercise? As the oldest child in her family, Kylie always felt she had to be the best at whatever she did. While growing up she could never quite measure up to her dad's expectations. No matter how well she did in school, he wanted her to do better. No matter how hard she tried to lose weight, he would tease her about her appearance.

Kylie's mother was an alcoholic, so she vowed to never touch that stuff. Instead she anesthetized her emotional pain with work and then with exercise. It's hard for someone like Kylie to do anything in moderation, especially something like exercise, which carries so many positive benefits.

Breaking the Exercise Fix

Like any other addiction, exercise needs to be done with self-control and balance. Kenneth Cooper, the father of aerobics, advises a 20-minute workout three or four times a week or every other day. Such a routine will enable a person to stay in shape. Those who go beyond his minimum recommendation usually do so for reasons other than good cardiovascular health.[8]

Exercise expert Richard Benyo suggests that those getting into a regular exercise routine can avoid an exercise addiction by following Cooper's recommendation. By keeping their exercise routine sensible they can get in shape, stay that way, and avoid the negative results of an addiction.[9]

If you feel you must build a more vigorous exercise routine, keep four things in mind:

* Build slowly.

* Get a checkup.

* Recognize your physical limitations.

* Prepare yourself emotionally and spiritually.

But just cutting back on the length and frequency of workouts won't solve the problem. There is an underlying drive that must be dealt with. Otherwise a person may simply temper exercise only to indulge in another addiction.

One way to prepare yourself emotionally and spiritually for exercise is by establishing goals. Identify why you're training. Determine how much weight you want to lose or how much time you want to spend exercising each week. Allow those goals to serve as parameters for your exercise routine.

While setting goals, remember that you are more than just a physical body. When Paul wrote to the Corinthians, he praised the discipline of the athlete who endured the rigors of training so he could accomplish his goal of winning a race or fight. But he also told the Corinthians that he disciplined his body so he could run the race of life without disqualification (1 Corinthians 9:24-27).

In addition to setting physical goals for yourself, set spiritual goals that will help you develop your mind and spirit. Determine to run the race of life with discipline and endurance.

As you set spiritual and emotional goals, you may discover that your exercise routine is crowding everything else out of your life. Here are three steps you can take to help you break your exercise fix.

Stop cold turkey. With most addictions, the only way to stop is to stop. If you've been working out regularly for a long time, such a thought may seem unrealistic. But it may be the only way you can get a handle on your life.

You probably have a long list of chores you have put off since you've been overexercising. Take a break from your exercise routine and catch up on your unfinished tasks. Near the end of your rest period, set some balanced goals for your exercise routine. Sit down with a friend and define what you think is reasonable for you. Ask for input from others.

Cut back. If stopping altogether isn't the best idea for you, reduce your exercise routine to something more balanced. Your schedule can include some races or competitions. But remember: You want to get a handle on your life. You must set some limits and abide by them.

Talk with someone who has worked through an exercise addiction. They can give you support as you try to gain control of your life.

Look deeper. Overcoming any kind of an addiction demands a look beyond the surface. Cutting back on your workout will help, but understanding what motivates the dragon within is crucial. If you don't look deeper than the symptoms you'll fall back into the same patterns or become trapped in another addiction. The final section of this book will help you gain the insight you need to put the dragon in his place.

▼

CHAPTER 8

Negativism— Feeling Good by Feeling Bad

Richard and Robert were identical twins. Both had brown eyes and black hair. Both stood four feet six inches tall. While the boys were identical in appearance, in other ways they were different, even opposite.

It was their ninth birthday, and the twins were excited about the surprise gifts they would receive from their parents. Since they were twins, they always received identical gifts.

To heighten the suspense on this birthday, the parents blindfolded Richard and led him into the barn where his gift was hidden. After the blindfold was removed, Richard's face clouded in disbelief. "A barn full of manure!" he said in disgust. "What kind of a present is this? Why did you give it to me? I deserve better."

He kicked the dirt. "What an awful present," he muttered. He dropped his head and trudged away.

The parents then brought Robert into the barn and took off his blindfold. He immediately grabbed a shovel and started digging. Thrilled beyond belief, he frantically hurled manure into the air.

Shocked by Robert's enthusiasm, his parents asked why

he was so excited. Stopping for a moment, the breathless boy exclaimed, "There's got to be a pony in here somewhere!"

This story illustrates the difference between a pessimist and an optimist, a person with a negative attitude and one with a positive attitude. Which child are you most like? Do you tend to assume the worst or look on the bright side of everything?

Nobody's a pessimist all the time. Most of us have a streak of negativism. That's not all bad. A touch of pragmatism sometimes prevents us from making foolish decisions.

Unfortunately, negativism can become an addiction. Some people are hooked on feeling bad, and since their problem is seldom addressed, they don't give much thought to getting free.

The Voice that Says "I Can't"

The word "negative" comes from the Latin word *negare*, meaning to deny. A negative person is one who consistently tells himself, "I can't, it won't work, it's not good enough." Every time a positive thought tries to emerge, the negative ones drive it right into the ground.

Negative-thinking defeatists have been pulled into a whirlpool of pessimistic attitudes, thoughts, words, and behaviors. They are convinced they can never do, become, or have anything worthwhile. And when they fail the inner voice says, "I told you so."

George Burns described a pessimist as "a man who feels bad when he feels good for fear he'll feel worse when he feels better." John Galsworthy observed that a defeatist is a person "who is always building dungeons in the air."

For "I can't" addicts, negativism is an orientation toward life. They look at life through a dark lens. Their outlook affects everyone they come in touch with. And the more intimate the relationship, the greater the pain.

Spouses and children of people hooked on negativism are generally filled with anger and resentment. Layers of gloom separate them from the ones they love. Family members eventually rebel against the daily reality of something always being wrong. They tire of the continual barrage of faultfinding, grumbling, murmuring, and complaining. They would like to get through just one day without hearing about poor health, a failing business, bad weather, lost friendships, and other negative aspects of life.

Getting High on Feeling Low

For years I wondered why some negative people I counseled found it so hard to gain freedom. They expressed a desire to get free, yet they seemed unable to wiggle off the hook. I began to wonder if these people were hooked on some kind of chemical released by their bodies during periods of negativism. The addiction seemed so severe I sensed something significant was involved.

Later I learned that experts make a distinction between *substance* and *process* addictions. *Substance addictions* refer to being hooked on external substances such as drugs, alcohol, nicotine, caffeine, and certain foods. *Process addictions* are addictions to a series of activities or interactions which hook a person and on which they become dependent.[1]

Some authorities believe that all addictions are substance addictions. Research indicates that eating disorders, preoccupation with certain sexual practices, workaholism, exercise, and even negativism have something in common with traditional addictions to alcohol or drugs.[2]

In the last chapter I pointed out that, during periods of extended running or aerobic exercise, the body releases natural pain-reducing and pleasure-producing substances. These opiate-like endorphins create a natural high that provides relief from anxiety while producing a sense of peace, well-being, and temporary euphoria.[3]

While more research is needed, some experts believe that the same thing happens when excessively negative persons criticize or judge themselves or others. Their negativism triggers the release of the same opiate-like endorphins a distance runner experiences and produces a rush of pleasurable feelings.

If this is true, it explains why defeatists have such a hard time breaking away from their negativism: They're addicted to the rush of negative excitement.[4]

Bob and Sandy came to me for counseling because Bob's negativism was destroying their marriage. "I never do anything right," Sandy cried. "I'm always wrong, and so are the kids. We hardly ever laugh anymore."

After several sessions I told Bob I thought he was hooked on negativism. I shared with him the possibility that he could be addicted to natural opiates released by his body during his periods of negativism. "You could actually be deriving a form of pleasure from your pessimism," I told him.

"That's ludicrous!" he said. "There's no way I get any pleasure out of being critical!"

"Being negative isn't pleasurable. But the feeling that's created as a result of the release of endorphins induces a state that's wonderfully awful. The next time you're criticizing your wife or children, check your metabolism. See if your pulse increases, your chest constricts, and you feel a warm rush through your body. See if you feel important and self-consumed. Check to see if you feel bad and good at the same time."

When we met the next week Bob was stunned by what he had experienced. "I did what you suggested," he said. "Sure enough, when I was feeling critical I noticed a rush of negative excitement and power. It reminded me of how I feel before I make an important presentation at work."

Realizing that feeling bad can sometimes feel good is a crucial step in overcoming addictive negativism. Accepting the possibility that negativism is both a process addiction and a substance addiction to a naturally-produced chemical helps explain why changing is so difficult.

There are other short-term "benefits" people hooked on negativism experience. For instance, when chronic pessimists are down on themselves, they reaffirm their belief that they are bad persons. Ironically, in so doing they prove to themselves that they aren't all bad. At least they feel they have enough insight to see their own hopeless situation!

Negativism is also a powerful tool used to control others. Just as a bucket of water can control a small fire, so critical people can exercise control over others with their fatalistic view of life. This power over people provides a sense of well-being as addicts pull others into their shadow.

Looking Back

Why are some people addicted to viewing life through a dark lens? In addition to the short-term physical and psychological benefits perpetuating this addiction, there are other causes which find their roots in the addict's family of origin.

Most of us tend to block out unpleasant memories from our childhood. We want to remember the best in our families. Consequently, we tend to believe our parents did a good job of parenting even if they didn't.

Usually, parents who fail at parenting didn't intend to hurt their children. More often than not they struggled because they had their own set of problems they were trying to work through. They may have been hounded by distortions they picked up from their parents. While they may have done the best job they could with their children, they passed down some of the consequences of their unhealthy behavior.

Overly negative people often grew up in dysfunctional families. In her book, *Negaholics*, Cherie Carter-Scott points out six characteristics of a dysfunctional family which give rise to addictive negativism.[5]

1. Love is conditional. "No matter what I did, it wasn't enough," Drew said. "My dad was a talented athlete and a successful businessman. He wanted me to be a chip off the old block. If I got a A- in school, he was disappointed it wasn't an A. If I got a double in a baseball game, he wanted a triple. I just never could measure up. Today I still hear Dad's voice. Even though I make a lot of money and have a great family, I always look at other people and feel I'm not good enough."

We all need to feel we are loved unconditionally. The apostle Paul wrote, "Love is patient" (1 Corinthians 13:4). The word he used for love, *agape*, is an unconditional love that patiently seeks what's best for the other person. An impatient love is self-serving.

Parents who love impatiently want to squeeze their child into a mold they've made. They demand the child change to please them. What happens when the child doesn't conform to the parent's expectations? The parent becomes irritated with the child's unchangeable traits.

Because Drew's dad insisted he live up to his standards, Drew never felt loved and accepted for who he was. He felt bad, not about things he had done, but about who he was.

Such feelings create shame at the core of our being. Our shame drives us to keep telling ourselves how worthless we are.

While each family is different, dysfunctional families love conditionally. Standards are established and love is dispensed according to how well each member performs against the standard. Negative people grow up feeling that they're never quite good enough.

2. Taboo topics can never be discussed. "It's just not something I'm comfortable talking about," Karen said. "Religion is a very private matter, and I don't believe people should discuss it."

Karen and Lyle had come to see me for premarital counseling. He was concerned because Karen seemed hypercritical of him. One subject which continually caused conflict was religion. She was irritated by the freedom with which he talked about God.

"Our family went to church every week," Karen said. "We believed in God, but religion and politics are two subjects we just didn't discuss."

In dysfunctional families, some subjects are off limits. Topics such as sex, religion, politics, money, relatives, addictions, illnesses, death, feelings, relationships, plans or activities, and the condition of a specific family member are never to be addressed.

Growing up under taboo topics feeds a shame-based personality. It makes children feel they are bad if they want to discuss such subjects—which, of course, they do.

3. Root family problems are not successfully discussed, dealt with, and resolved. Brian is the regional sales manager for one of our nation's largest airlines. He seems to have no problem communicating with the sales teams who work for him. He insists all interpersonal problems be settled between the people involved.

But his home life is a different story. He and his wife are on the verge of separation because she doesn't feel they ever resolve their disagreements.

"Brian, how did your family resolve problems when you were growing up?" I asked.

"We used to have some ferocious fights. Mom and Dad would get drunk and scream at each other. The kids would take sides, and it was all-out war. We said terrible things. Eventually, Dad would leave, slamming the door behind him. Mom would go into her room and pout. The next day Mom and Dad would be sober, and we all moved on with our lives like nothing ever happened. But we were a close, loving family, Bill. Even though we fought, there was a lot of love."

Few things create bitterness more quickly than unresolved family problems. That's why Paul told the Ephesians, "Do not let the sun go down while you are still angry" (Ephesians 4:26).

Anger needs to be expressed in a healthy way. Conflicts need to be resolved. When they aren't, a person grows up not knowing how to deal with negative emotions. Consequently, those emotions are stuffed inside and later expressed as extreme negativism.

4. Family secrets are guarded and passed on. Every family has a closet where it hides family secrets. These secrets may include a sexually-abusive family member, domestic violence, suicides, alcoholism, money issues, secret addictions, forms of mental illness which run in the family, or scores of other things.

Often these secrets have been passed down from one generation to another. Family members have silently agreed to an unwritten pact binding them to silence.

Because these secrets are hidden, they create shame. Tragically, this shame becomes the glue that bonds the family together. Each member instinctively knows that if the dark secrets are uncovered, the family will look bad.

Children may become critical of others in an effort to make their own shame seem not so bad. Or they might repeatedly tell themselves they are bad, unworthy persons since they come from a family with such a terrible past. Because dysfunctional families refuse to open the closet and turn on the lights, their shame is passed down from one generation to the next.

The apostle John urged us not to hide our sin and shame but to expose it to the light (1 John 1:7). Nothing destroys toxic shame like light.

5. Feelings are denied, avoided, discounted, and suppressed. My father always had a hard time talking about his feelings. I once asked him why. His answer revealed a lifetime of hurt and disappointment: "When the turtle's head gets stomped on, he don't stick it out of the shell no more."

Unfortunately, many children grow up in homes where they feel "stomped on" when they express their feelings. Some parents believe feelings are embarrassing, threatening, or disruptive. Feelings like anger, jealousy, and rejection are considered wrong.

But feelings are neither right nor wrong. They are an emotional response to the world around us. We need to avoid placing moral value on emotions. When we feel something, we need to identify the feeling and its cause. Then we can decide on an appropriate expression.

For instance, suppose a close friend hosts a party and doesn't invite you. The easiest response would be to simply stuff your hurt inside. But if you do that you'll form a judgment about your friend which may not be accurate. You might conclude that your friend doesn't enjoy your company. Later, that judgment will produce the negative belief that your friend is now your adversary.

Dealing with your feelings right away might involve mentioning them to your spouse or a friend. Your attitude would change quickly if the person you talked with reminded you that you weren't invited to the party because you told your friend you planned to be out of town that weekend.

In dysfunctional families, emotions aren't dealt with. Consequently, children grow up thinking their feelings are wrong, and they're ashamed to express them. Anger, jealousy, fear, and a host of other emotions are ignored and suppressed. These feelings pollute the soul and generate a negative self-concept which overflows into negative conversation.

Healthy families aren't afraid of the truth about their feelings. When emotions surface in an environment of love, they can be dealt with intelligently. Negative emotions can be flushed out in a non-damaging manner. Healthy emotions can be expressed.

Such communication demands a commitment to truth and love. The apostle Paul encouraged such openness when he exhorted the Ephesians to speak the truth in love (Ephesians 4:15).

6. Denial is normal. Earlier I mentioned how Brian and his family used to avoid dealing with root family problems. In our conversation I asked Brian if he ever thought that his family's manner of dealing with conflict seemed damaging.

"Oh, maybe a little," he answered. "But, like I said, we loved each other. Besides, when my parents were sober they were great to be around."

Not only did Brian deny the seriousness of the problems in his family, he glossed over them so they wouldn't look bad to others. He presented his family as a loving unit.

Since Brian had developed a sophisticated system of denial, he had a hard time admitting the seriousness of his negativism. He tended to ignore the fact that his critical attitude was destroying his wife and children.

Negative people believe their critical attitudes, actions, and conversations are justified. Their defense system is usually so hardened they think others just don't understand.

As long as people deny the problems, they won't take steps to correct them. The resulting toll is high. Families and friends suffer the constant barrage of pessimism, complaining, and critical conversations. Employers and fellow employees find their attitudes infected by the never-ending flow of down-talk from a person hooked on negativism.

These people need to be lovingly confronted with the seriousness and destructiveness of their addiction. As long as the problem is denied, they can't be healed. And neither can their families.

Finding the Missing Link

People who grow up in dysfunctional families sometimes

are hooked on pessimism. They may deaden their emotional pain by becoming hypercritical of themselves and others. They often believe they're bad, unworthy people. They constantly tell themselves, "I can't." Everything in life has a shadow cast over it.

Negative people tend to worry, feel sorry for themselves, judge others, find something wrong with even the best situations, and spout all kinds of reasons why something won't work.

Overcoming negativism involves identifying how you learned your "practiced" skills of negativism. Coming from a dysfunctional family doesn't excuse wrong attitudes and actions. But it is a major reason why you are that way today.

If you think you're hooked but aren't sure, ask a family member or friend. Listen to your self-talk for a few days. If you're still not sure, try to avoid all negative attitudes and conversations for a two-week period of time. If you can't, you're probably hooked. You may even discover you can't make it for a day.

If you'd like to better understand your negativism, work through the six characteristics of a dysfunctional family mentioned in this chapter. Think through your childhood to see if you can learn how your family of origin created an environment of shame, secrecy, denial, and suppressed emotions. Such self-discovery takes time and may be painful. But it's a crucial step.

No matter how long you've been negative, you can find freedom. As you look back and sort through some of your past problems, you will understand the cause of your shame. That's a crucial, ongoing process that will prepare you to begin to view yourself differently.

Counteracting the dark dragon in your soul will require additional insights and strategies. The final section of this book will provide some for you.

Further Help

For additional insights on addictive negativism, see:

Cherie Carter-Scott, *Negaholics* (Villard Books).

▼

CHAPTER 9

Workaholism— Getting High on Success

You wouldn't think something seemingly as insignificant as a gear-shift indicator could spell disaster for a car. But it can.

I used to own an Olds Cutlass that worked great except for the gear-shift indicator. When the indicator was on *N* the car was really in drive, not neutral. And when it was on *D* the car was really in second gear instead of drive.

One day I loaned the Olds to a friend and forgot to mention the car's one flaw. I was mowing the yard when Cindy, my wife, told me Kip wanted me on the phone. "He sounds upset," she said. I ran inside and picked up the phone.

"Bill," Kip said, breathing hard. "Billows of black smoke are coming out of the car's engine. And it's making a loud banging noise."

"What happened?" I asked.

"I don't know. I was just driving it down the freeway. I wasn't going any faster than you normally drive."

Actually, Kip hadn't done anything wrong. My car just couldn't handle traveling at 65 MPH in second gear.

I thought about my Olds the day I visited a man in my congregation who had just been admitted to the hospital. Jim classified his trip to the hospital as a precaution. In truth, he had suffered a minor heart attack.

For almost 10 years Jim had been racing through life at 65 MPH while in second gear. He said he had to live at full speed in order to build up his business.

I wondered how big Jim's business would have to get before he would shift gears. He already had one of the most successful sales forces in the state. He lived in a custom home on a wooded lot in an affluent suburb. Every year he bought a new $40,000 car.

Somehow, the baby blue hospital robe made him seem more human. The black bags under his eyes contained a sermon about the vices of workaholism. So did the heart monitor attached to his chest. I felt sorry for Jim and hoped he would listen.

I prayed with him that day. Later, I prayed with his family. The next day I visited Jim again. He looked better.

"Jim, you have to slow down," I urged.

"I can't," he said. "But I will start working out and watching what I eat."

"You're killing yourself," I said.

"I know. But it'll only be for awhile. Then I can slow down."

I wish I could say Jim has slowed down. He hasn't. Like millions of other people in our country, he's suffering from a potentially fatal addiction: workaholism.

A Squeaky-Clean Addiction

Author and business consultant Diane Fassel calls workaholism "the cleanest of all the addictions."[1] She observes that workaholism is socially promoted because it appears socially productive. People comfortably brag about being workaholics.

That's amazing! Can you imagine bragging about being hooked on gambling, drugs, or alcohol? Of course not.

But workaholism is viewed differently in our culture. Since success is a prized possession, that which seems to bring success can't be all bad. Indeed, some companies expect their employees to be workaholics.

But beware: Workaholism isn't just an addiction suffered by high-powered yuppy executives. No way! Housewives, students, ministers, policemen, and anyone else with a compulsion to work can become a workaholic.

Marks of a Workaholic

Enjoying work doesn't make someone a workaholic. Neither does working long hours. One key to identifying the problem is discovering how closely a person's sense of identity is tied to his work. There are several marks of a true workaholic.

The identity of workaholics is entirely wrapped up in their work. Take away their work and you take away their sense of value. Without work they feel worthless. Since their identity is measured by the quality and quantity of their work, workaholics move from one urgent project to another.

Workaholics never have time to relax. Driven by an inner need to produce, they find it hard to squeeze in time to play with their family or friends. Vacations are rare experiences for workaholics. When they do go on a vacation, it's often planned at the last minute because of their busy work schedule. Frequently they'll bring along a stack of work.

Workaholics are driven by a need to work as opposed to a healthy desire to be gainfully employed. Workaholics will sacrifice their health and families for the sake of their addiction with hardly a blink of remorse.

Driven by the belief that his work was important, Dr. Christiaan Barnard spent years developing the aortic heart valve. After successfully completing the first heart transplant, the South African surgeon became an overnight celebrity. His picture appeared in newspapers around the world. He made guest appearances on television talk shows. He was the epitome of success in the medical profession.

But there is another side to Dr. Barnard's story. In his book *One Life*, he tells how he sacrificed his family for his work. After being away from home four months he returned to a frigid greeting. "You wrote once a month to say you weren't coming home. That's what you wrote," his wife said.

"We were building valves—aortic valves," he replied.

"You were also building a family. I mean, once upon a time you were building one, until you dumped it into my lap."

As the two drove home, Dr. Barnard asked, "Why are you so upset?"

"Because we have ceased to exist for you," his wife answered.[2]

What a tragic story! Christiaan Barnard was a success in the eyes of the world. But he had failed his family. He took care of hearts around the world while neglecting those closest to him.

Workaholics deny there is a problem. People addicted to work admit they're workaholics, and some even brag about their work addiction.[3] But to them, being hooked on work is a virtue, not a problem. However, hard work is only a virtue when it is kept in balance with the rest of life.

The promise of financial and social benefits often blinds workaholics to the fact that they might be able to achieve those benefits apart from their compulsive work habits. They also fail to see the destructive consequences of their addiction.

Unfortunately, families of workaholics often enable them to continue with their addiction. "Phil's gone five days a week," Melissa told me. "I miss him. So do the kids. But we realize he travels because he loves us. He's given us a beautiful home and freedom from financial stress."

Her voice lowered, "I'm glad he doesn't drink or run around on me. Things could be a lot worse."

The real rub comes at her son's baseball games. Melissa sees other fathers cheering on their sons. Phil seldom makes it to a game. He's just too busy.

Melissa knows something is wrong with Phil, but she is afraid to surface the problem.

Workaholics are perfectionistic. Because workaholics measure their value by results, their work must be flawless.

Workaholics are frequently compulsive in their list-making. Their lists guard them against mistakes and give them a way of measuring their success. Lists are concrete expressions of perfectionism.

Several years ago I met a man who was a compulsive list-maker. John always carried a notepad. Whenever he had a thought about his work, he grabbed his pen. During meetings with his superiors he would pull out his lists and bring up countless irrelevant details. His perfectionistic attention to detail wasted time and distracted others from their work.

Workaholics are motivated by guilt. Many workaholics grew up in families where they weren't loved unconditionally. As children they often felt pressured to perform perfectly to be accepted. When they missed the mark, they coped with their guilt by trying harder the next time. Since they never resolved their guilt, it was suppressed.

As adults their buried guilt pushes them to work harder. Work deadens their emotional pain. It gives them hope that, with a little more effort, they'll be okay.

Marathon Workers and Sprinters

One common misconception about workaholism is that all workaholics fall into the same pattern. They don't.

Some workaholics work all the time. Like long-distance runners, they push themselves continually. A marathon worker will work six or seven days a week.

Rhonda has worked for the same company for 20 years without taking a single vacation. She's always the first person in the office each morning and the last to leave each night. Although she's only 50, Rhonda's doctors tell her she has the circulatory system of a 70-year-old. The constant stress has taken a high toll.

Why does she do it? When I asked her that question she said, "I felt as a woman I had to prove myself. And I made up my mind to do it no matter what the price."

Other workaholics work in binges. They remind me of sprinters who wait around a track meet for their event. Once the gun sounds they run full speed until the race is over.

During periods of intense work, sprinting workaholics labor for days at a time without rest. Occasionally they may go for weeks without much sleep. When the project is done, a blanket of depression often wraps itself around them. No wonder! During their work binge they experience an increase in adrenaline. While working so feverishly they feel they're doing something significant. They feel important. Afterwards they feel empty. To anesthetize the pain, they often start other projects.

Kelly writes commercials and short plays. He's one of the most talented artists I've ever known. He likes his work, and he especially enjoys working out of his home. Unfortunately, he puts his work off until the last minute.

One day he came to see me because his work schedule had him working all night and sleeping all day. He probably would have continued his lifestyle if it hadn't started taking a toll on his marriage.

Tall and handsome, Kelly plopped into a chair and crossed his arms. "I keep putting my writing jobs off until the night before they're due. I'm doing this every week, and it's killing me."

"Well, there has to be a reason. What is it?" I asked.

Kelly hadn't expected such a straightforward approach. He sat up in his chair and said, "I don't know."

The next week he came back with some answers.

"I think it gives me a rush to see if I can pull it off at the last minute," he said. Then he flashed his broad smile. "I kind of marvel at my own brilliance."

Kelly is hooked on the pressure, crisis, and the romance of getting the job done at the last minute. He loves feeling like the hero who rescued the damsel from an oncoming train just in the nick of time.

As you may have noticed, both Rhonda and Kelly are controlled by their jobs. Both have something to prove. Both work more than 60 hours a week. And both suffer because of their addiction.

Nobody's Perfect

If you're a workaholic, the natural high of meeting a challenge causes you to set increasingly higher goals for yourself. It's hard for you to imagine changing, because you believe life at a slower pace would be dull and the rewards wouldn't be as great. You probably also have a hard time believing you'd be okay if you and your work were less than perfect.

The truth is, neither you nor your work are perfect. Furthermore, your worth as an individual isn't determined by what you do, but by who you are. If you feel the only way to prove your worth is through your work, how will you know when you're okay?

Overcoming your workaholism begins with a recognition that you have value apart from your performance. Repeatedly the Bible states that God loves us for who we are instead of what we do. You are the handiwork of your Creator, who shaped you while you were in your mother's womb (Psalm 139:13-15).

Several years ago my wife and I were browsing through an art gallery in San Francisco. One particular sketch caught my eye. While I thought it unusual, the sketch didn't carry the appeal of many of the other works. Yet it was the most expensive piece in the gallery.

Curious, I looked closer. That's when I spotted the signature of the artist: Picasso.

The pencil sketch had value because of its creator. Similarly, you have value because you carry your Creator's signature.

The next time you find yourself getting pulled into a current of perfectionism, remind yourself:

- God loves me just like I am. I have value apart from my work.

- It's illogical for me to try and be perfect. Nobody except God is perfect.

- I don't have to be the one to do it all. God is in control. He carries the primary load. I share it with Him.

- I'm not inferior just because I make mistakes.

- Thank you, Lord, for making me like I am.

Overcoming False Guilt

Sometimes the driving emotional force in a workaholic's life is guilt. Guilt is the uncomfortable feeling we experience when we've done wrong. Unfortunately, all guilt isn't healthy or helpful. When we've really done something wrong, guilt is proper. It helps us make restitution and seek forgiveness. But many people experience guilt when they haven't done anything wrong. Such guilt results from misunderstanding or a misguided conscience.

Eric's parents were both doctors who wanted him to follow in their steps. Everything went great until Eric entered high school and started taking advanced math courses. He tried his best, yet he only made *B*'s. Each time his father looked at his report card he would shake his head and say, "You just have to work harder. You're not stupid. Lazy people never make anything of their lives."

Consequently, Eric believed that a hard-earned *B* was a sign of ignorance and laziness. He felt guilty every time he earned a *B* instead of an *A*.

Was his guilt valid? No! Eric hadn't done anything wrong. His conscience was misguided and overly sensitive. Years later as an adult, Eric has to deal with workaholism. His struggle for balance has forced him to reeducate his conscience. He had to realize that his parents had imposed on him unrealistic expectations and standards.

The next time you feel guilt motivating your rigorous work routine, ask yourself, "Why do I feel guilty?" Once you've identified the cause, ask yourself, "Is my guilt real or false?"

If it's real, develop a plan for dealing with it. If it's false, dismiss it as false and don't allow it to direct your life.

Grabbing What's Important

If you're a workaholic and I were to ask you, "Which is more important to you: making money or being devoted to your family?" without a moment's hesitation you'd probably answer, "My family."

But if I were to follow you around for a week, how would your actions answer that question? Would your life say that your work is more important than your family?

Of course, you'd justify your long hours by explaining that the money you hope to make will buy happiness for your family. But are you and your family happy now? Workaholics always seem to be chasing happiness. They hope to catch it down the road when they've achieved success.

But happiness isn't something that's achieved through hard work or money. The famed Irish poet and dramatist Oscar Wilde once wrote, "In this world there are only two tragedies. One is not getting what one wants, and the other is getting it." No matter how hard you may work at attaining success or how much success you attain, it won't satisfy.

The list of successful people who have self-destructed grows tragically long. When the veneer of achievement is stripped away, even those who are rich and powerful long for something more. In spite of all the evidence pointing to the fact that money and possessions can't satisfy, most of us don't get the picture.

Solomon said that nothing under the sun will give our lives lasting pleasure (Ecclesiastes 2:11). Fortunately, there's a God *above* the sun who can. The enjoyment of life is a gift from God. It's elusive if pursued apart from Him. When we focus on God, He fills us with joy regardless of our circumstances. No matter what we may have, if we have God we can enjoy life. Without Him, life is flavorless.

So Oscar Wilde wasn't completely right after all. There's a third tragedy greater than the two he mentioned: the tragedy of missing God!

Think about the futility of focusing your life on the pursuit of success and wealth. Even Solomon, the wealthiest man who ever lived, was wise enough to realize people leave this life exactly as they enter it: with nothing (Ecclesiastes 5:15).

Slow Down So Success Can Catch You

Such an insight could lead to despair. But there's an alternative. In Ecclesiastes 5:18-20, Solomon noted that God gives us three gifts.

- The ability to be satisfied with our work (v. 18).

- The ability to enjoy whatever wealth and possessions we have (v. 19). He enables us to say, "If what I have now is all I'm ever going to have, it's enough. I'm satisfied."

* The ability to be so occupied with living that we haven't time to be miserable (5:20). Rather than racing through life to some unknown destination, God enables us to enjoy life.

A pastor once asked a prominent member of his congregation, "Whenever I see you, you're always in a hurry. Your wife tells me you're always working. Tell me, where are you running all the time?"

The man answered, "I'm running after success, fulfillment, and the reward for all my hard work."

The pastor responded, "That's a good answer if you assume that all those blessings are somewhere ahead of you trying to elude you and that if you run fast enough you might catch up with them. But isn't it possible that those blessings are behind you looking for you and that the more you run the harder you make it for them to find you?"

Isn't it possible that God has all sorts of wonderful presents for you? Take a look at the Christmas tree He offers.

*

Joy
Waves
Sunsets
Fall leaves
Spring flowers
Laughing children
The embrace of love
Moments of reflection

There really is more to life than work. Indeed, joy is a butterfly that flys away when you chase it. But when you stand still, it lands on your shoulder. By slowing down and focusing on the simple things of life, one day you'll discover that joy has found you.

If you're chasing hard after fulfillment through work, I hope you see the danger. I hope you want freedom. If you do, move ahead into Part Three and we'll take the next step together.

Further Help

Diane Fassel, *Working Ourselves to Death* (Harper Collins Publishers).

Frank Minirth, Paul Meier, Frank Wichern, Bill Brewer, States Skipper, *The Workaholic and His Family* (Baker Book House).

Part Three

▼

Overcoming
Fatal
Attractions

▲

▼

CHAPTER 10

The Power of Admitting You're Helpless

On my eighth birthday my parents gave me a beautiful BB gun with a wooden stock. While I enjoyed shooting cans and bottles, birds were my favorite target.

One afternoon I raised my gun and aimed at a bird perched in the willow tree in our back yard. Just as I was about to squeeze the trigger, my older sister, Patsy, ran into the yard waving her arms and yelling.

As the bird flew away she looked at me and smiled as if to say, "There, I showed you!"

In that moment something inside of me took control. I lowered the gun and aimed at a part of my sister's anatomy designed for sitting. She took off at a full run. But she didn't run fast enough. I pulled the trigger and the BB caught up with her. She darted into the house crying and screaming, "I've been shot! I've been shot!"

For a moment I wondered what made me do something like that. I even wondered why I enjoyed it so much.

As my dad prepared to spank me in the same spot I had shot my sister, I did everything I could to convince him Patsy deserved what she got. When that didn't work, I promised I'd reform. I hoped my tears would cause my dad to say, "Hey, it was a freakish act. He'll never do it again. I won't spank him."

But Dad spanked me anyway. And he took away my gun. Yet he wasn't able to take away the dark creature in my heart who enjoyed doing bad things.

I remember as a kid making up my mind to be good. But no matter how hard I tried, I still did things I shouldn't have done. As I matured I learned how to cover my tracks. But even though others didn't know what was going on in my life, I knew.

When I was 20 years old I had a serious problem with alcohol and drug abuse. There was a power within me I couldn't control. No matter how determined I was to overcome it, I always lost.

Finally, on the verge of a mental breakdown, I gave up the battle. With nowhere to turn, I cried out to God. I acknowledged my inability to overcome the dark force within me and begged God to deliver me.

I took the first step. I admitted my helplessness.

You Can't Swim with Waders On

If you've identified an addiction in your life and you want to work through it by yourself, this chapter will help you realize you can't. The first step in finding freedom from your addiction is admitting your helplessness to do so alone.

Several years ago a fisherman in Oregon drowned when he lost his footing, fell into the current, and was swept into deep water. His companion said his friend would have made it safely to shore if the waders he was wearing hadn't filled with water. The victim was an excellent swimmer and knew what to do in deep water. But something strong and heavy pulled him under.

Like that fisherman, we often know the right thing to do about our addictions. We may even vow to do it. But we can't. Our problem is we're slaves to our lower nature. Doing what's right is like trying to swim while wearing water-filled waders.

Even the most mature people struggle with their lower nature. For instance, few people love God more than the apostle Paul did. Yet Paul confessed, "I do not understand what I do. For what I want to do I do not do, but what I hate I do" (Romans 7:15).

Paul experienced relentless warfare. He loved God and wanted to obey the laws of God. He longed for spiritual victory. But he found himself repeatedly doing things he despised. Instead of feeling free he felt enslaved to his sinful appetites.

If you're hooked on food, sex, gambling, helping, or a host of other things, you know about slavery. You know how it feels to obey the commands of a master who demands your submission.

The Dragon Awakens

The most significant thing that occurs in the initial stage of an addiction is the emergence of your sinful, addictive personality. Like a hibernating dragon, it awakens and takes control.

The dragon was there all along. But it was waiting for the right stimulus to shake it out of its slumber. Our problem is we aren't masters in our own home. We're the slaves. Our sinful nature has taken over. As Paul observed his own behavior, he concluded, "It is no longer I myself who do it, but it is sin living in me" (Romans 7:17).

When Paul referred to himself as "I," he spoke of his core personality, that part of him which sought after God. He spoke of that place in his personality where God's Spirit lived.

Paul knew that his true self, the part of himself that was united with Christ, wasn't carrying out the wrong behavior. Instead it was his sinful propensity and its dragon-like appetites.

Don't misunderstand what Paul meant. He wasn't justifying his wrong actions. Nor was he shifting responsibility away from himself. Instead, he was stating a fact. The true Paul, who so desired to do right, wasn't the one doing the evil. Instead it was the dragon who had gained dominion over him.

While I know Paul didn't have an addiction, like everyone else he had the potential for one (1 Corinthians 6:12,13). Even though he kept his sin under control, it continually tried to dominate him. He knew that the dragon within had the power to make him a prisoner. In fact, he said he knew what it was like to be its prisoner (Romans 7:23).

Wet Paint—Do Not Touch!

You might think knowing the right thing to do will help you avoid your addiction. It doesn't. In the garden, Eve knew what God wanted from her. But Satan actually used the commandment of God to tempt her. He asked her, "Did God really say . . . ?" (Genesis 3:1). That question was the starting place of her temptation.

Few things stir up our sinful appetites like the word "forbidden." For instance, what do you instinctively want to do when you see a sign that says, "Wet Paint—Do Not Touch!"? I know what I want to do. I want to disobey that rule. I want to touch the paint to see for myself if it's wet.

Nothing excites the dragon in your soul like a rule declaring something off limits. That's why the dragon uses the laws of God to gain dominion over your life. The law will remind you that God said gluttony, lust, dishonesty, and a host of other things are wrong. You'll look at the commandments and know what you should do. You'll even tell yourself you're going to do the right thing. When you do, the part of you that wants to do right enters hand-to-hand combat with your sinful nature. And you don't have a chance.

Does this mean God's law is bad? Does it mean good rules are really harmful since they stir up our sinful appetites? Not at all. Paul said it simply shows how evil the dragon is. If it can use something as good as the laws of God to motivate us to do evil, what is below it? (Romans 7:13,14). Regardless of how spiritual you may be, once the dragon within you is awakened it will do anything it can to bring you into submission.

Paul realized our sinful natures want one thing: *total control of our lives* (Romans 7:23). The dragon wants to embrace its idol and can only do so if it controls our lives. Because the dragon is so powerful, you're incapable of controlling it on your own. Remembering the right thing to do only excites it. Vowing to do what's right feeds it. The more you try to resist, the more certain your fall.

Do you now see why an addiction is so enslaving? The dragon is ruthless and powerful. It even uses good intentions and godly laws to draw you into a losing battle.

A Dog Is a Dog and a Dragon Is a Dragon

Since you can't beat the dragon, maybe you think you can pacify it. Perhaps you want to reform it like you would a household pet. You'd better forget it.

A playful, buff-colored Cocker Spaniel named Pumpkin graced the Perkins' household for 13 years. Over those years I taught Pumpkin all kinds of tricks. She obeyed the common commands like sit, lie down, and roll over. I also trained her to jump through a hoop, close a door, sit on her hind legs, and fall over as though dead when I shot her with an imaginary gun.

Yet in spite of all my training, I couldn't keep Pumpkin from acting like a dog. She always did doggy things. She ate things that people tried not to step in. She sniffed other dogs in places only dogs sniff. She went to the bathroom in public. I could have dressed her in clothes, as my sons did on occasion, but she would still be a dog.

Similarly, your sinful propensity doesn't reform when you enter a church. It doesn't change when you come to faith in

Christ. You can go to church, read your Bible, pray daily, and even lead a ministry without reforming your sinful nature. Paul said, "I know that nothing good lives in me, that is, in my sinful nature" (Romans 7:18).

When we come under the domination of our dragon, we're capable of doing anything evil, whether we're believers or not. When controlled by the dragon, we can no more do good than a dog can talk.

Yet when wrestling with the dragon, people often think they can win. They deny the dragon is awake. They tell themselves, "If I just feed it this once, it will go back to sleep." And when it does take a brief nap, they think they've got it licked. They don't know it yet, but when the dragon awakens it will be stronger than ever.

Fighting a Losing Battle

Rocco Francis Marchegiano was the original "Rocky." He won 49 fights in 10 years—43 by knockout. Marchegiano never lost a fight. He's the only heavyweight champion who can make that boast. Anybody who climbed in the ring with Rocky was fighting a losing battle.

In a similar vein, every time you try to fight your addiction alone, you're destined to lose. You're fighting an opponent you simply can't beat. Paul wrote:

> It seems to be a fact of life that when I want to do what is right, I inevitably do what is wrong. I love to do God's will so far as my new nature is concerned; but there is something else deep within me, in my lower nature, that is at war with my mind and wins the fight and makes me a slave to the sin that is still within me. In my mind I want to be God's willing servant but instead I find myself still enslaved to sin (Romans 7:21-23, TLB).

Paul's words remind me of a poem I found several years ago. It describes the struggle and defeat we experience when we fight against our addictions alone. While I don't know who wrote it, it's entitled, "The Yipiyuk."

> In the swamplands long ago,
> Where the weeds and mudglumps grow,
> A Yipiyuk bit on my toe...
> Exactly why I do not know.
> I kicked and cried And hollered "Oh!"
> The Yipiyuk would not let go.
> I whispered to him soft and low.
> The Yipiyuk would not let go.
> I shouted "Stop," "Desist" and "Whoa."
> The Yipiyuk would not let go.
> Yes, that was 16 years ago,
> And the Yipiyuk still won't let go.
> The snow may fall, the winds may blow.
> The Yipiyuk will not let go.
> I drag him 'round each place I go,
> And now my child at last you know
> exactly why I walk so slow.

Like the Yipiyuk, your sinful nature will resist letting go. For awhile you may try to ignore it. Later you may insist it doesn't really have a hold on you. But if you hope to break its power you must first realize it's there and admit you don't have the power to dislodge it.

Hopefully, you'll tire of fighting a losing battle. Paul did. In desperation he cried out: "Oh, what a terrible predicament I'm in! Who will free me from... this deadly lower nature?" (Romans 7:24, TLB).

Like Paul, we must realize the uselessness of struggling against our addiction. If you see your powerlessness and sense your need for the Dragonslayer, continue on with me. In the next chapter we'll enter the dragon's lair.

▼

CHAPTER 11

The Freedom
of Living
Without Shame

Hidden away in a far cor-
ner of your mind is a
dark cave. You try to forget it's there. But you can't.

Occasionally you look inside. A tide of fear rises and you
retreat. Fear keeps you away from the cave.

Sometimes you see smoke spiraling upward from the dark
opening. It reminds you that the dragon is still there.

The dragon, your sinful nature, keeps your shame alive. It
carries memories of the horrible things that happened to you
during your childhood. It represents all the terrible things
you've done to others.

The dragon carries your family secrets, those things
every family member knows about but refuses to mention.

- Secrets about physical and sexual abuse.

- Secrets about alcoholism and brutal family fights.

- Secrets about other addictions and the grave consequences that flow from them.

- Secrets about imperfections you never talk about.

The dragon embodies all your insatiable appetites, the

ones no amount of food, sex, alcohol, gambling, working, helping, or spending can satisfy. The dragon is your addictive personality. It is your sinful propensity, the part of you that craves an idol.

The dragon within is the reason you feel you're a bad, unworthy person. The dragon is the reason you don't believe anyone would love you if they really knew you. The fear that keeps you away from the cave is what causes you to keep others away. If they saw deep inside you they'd see the dragon. The people you value would think less of you. You could lose your only chance for intimacy.

For years you've tried to fight the dragon alone. Hopefully by now you've surrendered. You realize you can't slay it by yourself.

You Can't Starve a Dragon

Unfortunately, many recovery programs fight the dragon by denying it food. They specialize in abstinence. Certainly it's crucial for you to stop your addictive behavior. But starving the dragon isn't enough. He won't shrivel up and die. He'll only hibernate until something else comes along that appeals to him.

As long as the shame which feeds our poor sense of identity remains untouched, we're vulnerable to other addictions. We have to deal with the shame. We must walk into the cave and face the dragon. There's no other way.

Such a thought is terrifying. It means exposing to the light all the shameful things about ourselves and our family. It means running the risk of rejection.

Shame-filled people won't open up in a hostile environment. Consequently, many religious people play make-believe. They pretend the dragon is in its cave sleeping when in reality it's in control of their lives. They work hard at projecting a false image of purity and togetherness.

Dealing with your sinful nature demands brutal honesty. It means exposing all your shame to the light. It's hard to tell another person about your dragon, so I encourage people to begin by telling God. He's the Dragonslayer. Paul knew it. After describing his losing battle he exclaimed, "Who will free me from my slavery to this deadly lower nature? Thank God! It has been done by Jesus Christ our Lord. He has set me free" (Romans 7:25, TLB).

I'm fascinated that, after giving thanks to God for rescuing him, Paul didn't immediately focus on his new-found victory. Instead he spoke about God's deliverance and acceptance. He wrote, "There is now no condemnation for those who are in Christ Jesus" (Romans 8:1). God saw the dark side of Paul and loved him anyway.

The apostle's words give me hope. They tell me that God will also accept me despite all the things I have hidden in the cave.

Melted Heroes

Dr. Paul Brand tells a story that gives us some insight into dealing with the shame of our sinfulness.

During World War II the English people suffered greatly. At one point German bombers attacked London for 57 consecutive nights with raids lasting as long as eight hours. Fifteen hundred planes dropped bombs every night. The only thing that gave the people hope was the courage of the Royal Air Force pilots who flew into the skies each day to battle the Germans.

The people of London adored these pilots. Winston Churchill expressed the feelings of the citizens when he said, "Never in the history of human conflict has so much been owed by so many to so few." When these pilots walked down the streets of London decked out in their uniforms, the people treated them like gods. Girls craved their attention. Children touched them.

Unfortunately, some of the pilots returned from the war not looking like gods. One of the planes they used, the Hurricane, an agile, effective British fighter, had a fatal design flaw. The single-propeller engine was mounted in front, a scant foot or so from the pilot, with fuel lines snaking alongside the cockpit. When the plane was hit, the exploding fuel lines immediately engulfed the cockpit with flames. The pilot might eject, but in the one or two seconds it took him to find the lever the fire in the cockpit melted off the features of his face: nose, eyelids, lips, and often cheeks.

Plastic surgeons performed miracles of reconstruction on the faces of the men caught in this inferno. But even with the best of care the burned fliers left the hospital with terribly scarred faces. They were no longer handsome. To the outside world they were freaks.

Understandably, these brave warriors feared rejection.

- Would any woman love them?

- Would employers want a freak working for them?

- Would their friends socialize with them?

Some of these men suffered intense emotional pain from their physical injuries. Their families couldn't accept their new faces. Wives slowly withdrew and then divorced their scarred husbands. These men stayed indoors, refusing to venture outside except at night.

Pilot Peter Foster was more fortunate. His girlfriend assured him that she loved him regardless of his scarred face. The two were married before he left the hospital.

Peter said that his wife became his mirror. She saw his ugly face and loved him anyway. When she smiled at him, he knew he was okay.[1]

A Light in the Cave

What Peter Foster experienced with his wife, Paul experienced with God. God saw Paul's ugly, sinful nature and loved him anyway.

Recognizing God's acceptance is crucial if we're going to experience freedom from our addictions. The healing of shame begins when we look our sin full in the face, acknowledge it, and bring it into God's presence. Here's an exercise I'd like you to try which will help you take these steps.

Find a quiet place where you'll be undisturbed. Take three or four minutes to quietly commune with the Lord Jesus. Because Jesus has promised never to leave us or forsake us, this is more than just an exercise. You are allowing the Lord to penetrate the darkest corners of your heart.

Now picture the cave in the corner of your mind. Begin walking toward it remembering that Jesus is at your side. As you enter the cave, the light of the Lord's presence fills every corner of the cave (1 John 1:7). No longer can the dragon hide. He is exposed to the full light of the Lord's glory. Every shameful family secret is exposed. Every shameful thing you've ever experienced is there for Him to see.

You may think Jesus is going to reject you because of what He sees in your life. Yet instead of turning away in disgust, Jesus walks closer to your dragon. He gazes at all the things you're ashamed to even think about. He examines the reasons you feel unworthy of love.

At this point, review the shameful secrets you're hiding. Think about the shameful experiences you've had.

What does Jesus say to us as we face our secrets with Him? He opens His arms wide and says, "Come to me."

With His arms wrapped around you, He softly tells you, "I see it all, and I love you. I see it all, and I accept you. All you've shown me I carried away. It was nailed to a cross with Me."

Receiving God's acceptance is crucial. Nothing can take the place of unconditional love. His acceptance is far better than any pleasure our addictions offer. He provides us with authentic intimacy that exposes the illusion of intimacy offered by our addictions. His acceptance and forgiveness demonstrate the wonder of His grace. They diminish the pain of our shameful secrets, pain we feel compelled to deaden with addictive behavior.

Accept Yourself as God Does

Most of us have some negative feelings about ourselves. If you've done nothing to heal your shame, you'll experience an intense fear of rejection that will hinder your progress. It will keep you from becoming intimate with God and other people.

Since shame is at the core of addictive behavior, it's crucial for you to counteract your negative feelings about yourself. Doing so is a choice. You can choose to say, "God unconditionally loves me, and I receive His love and love myself." Whenever you're alone, say it out loud. Say it often!

Naturally, the dragon will fight this. It wants to cut you off from the only love that will satisfy. It wants you to wallow in shame, desperately seeking love in addictive behavior.

You may know of things you do that make you unworthy of God's love. Of course! We all do wrong things. But God loves you for who you are. *He loves you!* Paul wrote that Christ died for us while we were sinners (Romans 5:8). He didn't demand a change on our part before extending His love. He loves us in spite of what we do.

There is nothing you can do to make yourself more lovable to God! You are loved just as you are. If you refuse to believe you're loved, then you're calling God a liar. You are implying that you can determine your value better than God can. Are you ready to say that? I hope not.

Saying, "God loves me and I accept His love" counteracts the voice of shame. God's love has the power to transform your life.

I recently talked with a talented woman who is a friend of mine. Since childhood she's struggled with an eating addiction. She said she never felt worthy of love. Driven to earn love, she dressed well and worked hard. Occasionally, when she felt overwhelmed with feelings of shame, she'd binge.

I've noticed that she has a hard time accepting compliments. When I asked her why, she said, "I feel people only like me for what I do. If they knew the real me, they wouldn't accept me. Since I realize they don't know the real me, I reject their compliments."

My friend's problem was immediately thinking of the bad things she had done whenever people complimented her. She looked at the dragon instead of at the Lord. She knew her dragon didn't deserve any praise. But her friends were appreciating her, the real her. They loved her in spite of the dragon.

Overcoming her feelings of shame demands that she focus on God's unconditional love for her. She needs to see and accept herself as God does.

Accepting God's love and allowing Him to change your self-image is a free choice. You can choose to flood your mind with shameful thoughts that cloud your identity as someone God loves. Or you can say, "God loves me and I am His child." As you begin to acknowledge God's love, you will begin to see yourself as He does.

A Powerless Dragon

One thing you can do to enhance a healthy self-love and promote the healing of your shame is to realize that the dragon's power over you has been broken. You don't have to listen to its lies. You don't have to allow its shame-filled words to control your thoughts and actions.

Please don't misunderstand. I didn't say the dragon is dead. It isn't. As long as you live your lower nature will be around to tempt you. But its power has been broken. The realization of this fact was one of the great learning experiences of my life.

Paul made reference to this truth when he wrote, "Through Christ Jesus the law of the Spirit of life set me free from the law of sin and death" (Romans 8:2). When Paul used the word "law" he wasn't referring to a rule or regulation. Instead, he was speaking of a principle. The principle of sin and death is simply that sin and death always pull us down. They always compel us to do wrong.

The principle of the Spirit of life speaks of the new life God has given us through Christ's Spirit. His life liberates us from the downward pull of sin.

The principle of sin and death is like the law of gravity. You may deny the law of gravity. But proving its validity is easy. All you have to do is jump off a diving board. You may spring high in the air as you catapult off the end of the board, but a moment later you'll be going down.

For years mankind was enslaved to the law of gravity. We were powerless to overcome its downward pull. But on December 17, 1903, two bicycle mechanics, Orville and Wilbur Wright, piloted their plane into the sky. The laws of aerodynamics they employed demonstrated that gravity could be overcome.

Similarly, many people doubt that the dragon's power can be broken. Yet as the laws of aerodynamics, when applied properly, liberate airplanes from the downward pull of gravity, so God's Spirit frees us from the gravity of sin. He liberates us from our sinful appetites.

It's urgent that you begin to understand and experience the Spirit's freedom. Why? Because too many recovery programs trade one form of addictive behavior for another. They don't offer the insight you need to be liberated from your dragon. It's time for you to break free of the vicious cycle. Your freedom is there for the taking.

In the next chapter you will further understand how you can find the new, liberated you.

▼

CHAPTER 12

Devoted to the Dragonslayer

I'm a barefoot water skier. I love the exhilaration of skimming across glassy-smooth water at high speeds. I love the spray of water at my sides. And I love the challenge of performing tricks without skis.

Over the years I've had numerous friends ask, "Bill, could you teach me to water ski barefooted?"

I always answer the same way: "If you're willing to repeatedly fall face-first while racing over the water at 40 MPH, I can teach you."

Giving up an addiction is like learning how to barefoot water ski. A person must be willing to experience a little pain. Stopping an addiction hurts. The pain may be physical, emotional, or both, but it's real.

Yet the simple fact is that nobody ever found freedom from an addiction without stopping the addictive behavior. As we deal with our shame and strengthen our understanding of what it means to be a child of God, we must also stop acting out the addictive behavior.

The Law of Human Gravity

In his book *Addictive Thinking*, Dr. Abraham Twersky

137

observes that there is a law of human behavior that seems as inviolable as the law of gravity. He calls it the law of human gravity.

The law states, "A person gravitates from a condition that appears to be one of greater distress to a condition that appears to be one of lesser distress, and never in the reverse direction." This law maintains that it's impossible for a person to choose the greater distress.[1]

Most of my friends weren't willing to learn how to barefoot water ski because for them the distress of falling at 40 MPH was greater than the distress of failing to learn. Several of them gave up after smacking the water face-first five or six times.

But some have learned. They fell as many as 15 times before they succeeded. Yet they didn't give up. Why? Because for them the distress of failure was greater than the pain of falling.

Since it's painful for any of us to stop an addiction, why would we be willing to undergo the pain? Why would we give up the pleasure derived from the addiction?

First, we will want to quit when the physical and emotional pain of continuing our addictive behavior reaches disastrous proportions. Such things as hangovers, hallucinations, falls and bruises, and the loss of employment, family, and friends could make an alcoholic give up drinking. People with food, sex, helping, or gambling addictions all eventually experience their hellish consequences. When that happens, they want out.

Second, we may stop our addictive behavior when we see that the rewards of abstinence are greater than the pleasures of the addiction.[2] I was willing to undergo the pain of whacking my face against the water while learning how to barefoot water ski. Why? Because I had visions of myself skiing across the lake with rooster tails of water flying up behind me. I could see myself crossing the boat's wake without skis. I could hear the praise of my friends.

With such rewards in view I gladly suffered the pain of repeated failure. Eventually, my determination paid off.

Make a List and Check It Twice

If you asked a counselor to help you break free from your addiction, he or she might ask you to perform the simple exercise outlined below. I also suggest you complete these steps.

First, make a list of the consequences of continuing with your addictive behavior. Imagine what would happen to you if you didn't stop and no one made you stop. Your list should include consequences you've already suffered. It should also describe the worst-case scenario at each level for not stopping. Use the following format to complete your list.

Consequences of My Addiction

1. To my family...
2. To my employment...
3. To my health...
4. To my reputation...
5. To my self-image...
6. To my finances...
7. To my future...

Most people who struggle with an addiction reach points of desperation in their lives. These may be precipitated by tragedies or crises such as losing a job or separating from a spouse due to an addiction. Occasionally, the fear of death or disease may drive addicts to this point of despair. Sometimes these repeated failures serve as a wake-up call. The wreckage of broken relationships may force addicts to want to find freedom.

The purpose of the list is to help you see that the pain of your addiction is greater than the pain of stopping. It's aimed at helping you say, "Enough is enough. I've had it. I want freedom."[3]

Second, make a similar list describing the benefits you and those you love would experience if you stopped your addictive behavior. This list will reveal the rewards of abstinence.

Benefits of My Abstinence

1. To my family...
2. To my employment...
3. To my health...
4. To my reputation...
5. To my self-image...
6. To my finances...
7. To my future...

Take some time right now to complete these lists. Use the topics suggested as starting points. Add others that may apply to you.

After completing your lists, prayerfully consider which description you would prefer to characterize your life. Which promises the lesser distress? Which offers greater joy?

Perhaps you've already chosen to stop your addictive behavior. Your choice involves turning *away* from those things that are destroying your life. But it also means turning *to* something. To be free of your secret addiction you must turn to God and give Him your life.

Burning Your Ships

When the Spanish explorer Hernando Cortez landed at Vera Cruz, Mexico, in 1519, he was intent on conquest. To ensure the devotion of his men, Cortez set fire to his fleet of 11 ships. With no means of retreat Cortez's army had only one direction to move: into the Mexican interior. Cortez understood the price of commitment and he paid it.

The apostle Paul also understood the price of dedication. After assuring us of our victory in Christ, he calls on us to burn our ships, bridges, or anything else that ties us to our destructive former life. Furthermore, he challenges us to commit ourselves completely to God: "Therefore, I urge you brothers in view of God's mercy to offer your bodies as living sacrifices, holy and pleasing to God. This is your reasonable act of worship" (Romans 12:1, my translation).

Is Paul asking a lot? Yes! But he's not asking too much. He begins his exhortation with the word "therefore" because he wants to point us back to everything he's written in the previous 11 chapters. In those chapters he explained that God offers us forgiveness, acceptance, freedom from the dragon, a wonderful future, and the power needed for a victorious life. In light of all that, God wants our total devotion.

Earlier I mentioned that Paul found victory over his dragon through his relationship with Christ. To experience his victory, he had to be willing to devote himself completely to God.

It's important to realize that God will forgive and accept us whether or not we give our entire selves to Him. He extends His mercy without strings to all who believe (Ephesians 2:8,9).

But our refusal to devote ourselves to God short circuits His power in our lives. As long as we cling to our addictive behavior, we alienate ourselves from the One who has the power to help us.

It's the Reasonable Thing to Do

For a couple of years after I became a Christian I struggled with this whole idea of dedication. Often the setting in which I saw people being exhorted to devote themselves to God was filled with emotion. Unfortunately, emotionally-generated decisions usually evaporate when the emotions disappear.

Paul told the Romans that their act of commitment was to be reasonable. In the original language, reasonable meant a decision based on logic. In light of the terrible consequences of continuing on with an addiction, in light of the benefits of abstinence, and in light of all of the gifts God offers through Christ, the only logical thing to do is devote ourselves completely to God.

Obviously, such an act can't be forced. God doesn't hold a gun to our heads and demand our devotion. As anyone who has tried to help an addict can testify, addicts won't stop their destructive behavior until they are ready to do so. That's why Paul urged us to offer ourselves to God.

When we enter into a committed relationship with God, He begins to change us. Part of that change occurs after He has allowed us to discover we can't make it without Him. At about the same time we also begin to realize what He offers us. Once we come to those two realizations, He doesn't have to force us to commit ourselves to Him. It's obviously the reasonable thing to do. He brings us to the place where we want give ourselves to Him.

Saying "I Do" to God

I have a friend who fell in love with a beautiful and charming woman. After they dated for six months, he wanted to propose to her. But he kept thinking of all kinds of reasons for *not* marrying her.

- What about children? Will I be a good dad?
- What about my friends? Will they like her?
- What about her family? Will they accept me?
- What about money? Will we be able to make it?

Over and over we reviewed each of his questions. Each time he concluded that the positives outweighed the negatives. Yet he was hesitant to make the commitment. Meanwhile, his girlfriend patiently waited.

Finally he concluded he couldn't live without her, so he proposed marriage and committed himself by saying "I do."

Our relationship with God is much like a marriage. At some point we must step up to the altar and say "I do." We must choose to devote ourselves to Him alone.

Cultivating Your Spiritual Life

While such a decision of devotion to God occurs only once, it's usually renewed numerous times. As a pastor I've had the privilege of performing ceremonies for married couples who wanted to formally renew their commitments. In some cases they did so to break with an incidence of infidelity so they could move forward with their marriage.

Similarly, if you devote yourself completely to God, you may stray from Him. Maybe you have strayed from Him in the past. You can't *redo* your original commitment, but you can *renew* it. This is a crucial step in nurturing your spiritual life and finding freedom from your secret addiction.

Because an addiction is a spiritual problem, it isolates us from our inner self, from God, and from other people. The longer an addiction continues, the more spiritually isolated we become. When the dragon is in full control of our lives we are unable to connect with God or others. Sin aims to kill us, smother our personalities, and destroy our spiritual lives.

In the early stages of an addiction, the idol seems to nurture life and bring fulfillment to our inner selves. But as the addiction progresses, the nurturing proves to be a mirage. That's why, as an addiction continues, a spiritual withering occurs. For healing to occur, we must recommit ourselves to God and cultivate our spiritual lives.

Our willingness to grab hold of an idol in the form of an addiction shows our need for God. It reveals the hunger in our soul for something outside ourselves. Saint Augustine wrote about this hunger centuries ago: "Our hearts were made for you, O Lord, and they are restless until they find their rest in you."

Paul wants us to allow God to give us this rest. He wants us to experience union with God so we can grow spiritually. That's why he exhorts us to offer our bodies to God as living sacrifices.

If you'd like to dedicate yourself to God, I'd encourage you to do so now. Perhaps it would help for you to return to the scene described in the last chapter. Picture yourself with the Lord Jesus after He has seen all of your shameful secrets and assured you of His forgiveness.

In the last chapter you heard His words of acceptance. Now is the time for you to accept Him. Thank Him for carrying away your guilt. Express your faith in His resurrection. Now name each member of your body, including your mind, which you want to give to Him. As you hand yourself over to the Lord, you're choosing to serve Him rather than an addictive idol.

When we offer ourselves to God we're placing our lives in His hands. Unlike the animal sacrifice offered by the ancient Jews, we're to present ourselves to God as *living* sacrifices. Our bodies are to be given to Him for His use. Such an act is not only reasonable, it's deeply spiritual. We are to live our lives for Him and allow Him to live His life in us. In so doing we find strength for stopping our addictive behavior.

Renewing Your Mind

Once you make the decision to stop your addictive behavior and hand your life over to God, you'll face a period of intense struggle. The dragon won't let you go without a fight. The world, the flesh, and the devil will pressure you to return to your worldly behavior.

That's why Paul exhorts us, "Don't copy the behavior and customs of this world, but be a new and different person with a fresh newness in all you do and think. Then you will learn from your own experience how his ways will really satisfy you" (Romans 12:2, TLB).

No longer are you to allow your addictive environment to mold your life as it once did. Instead you must experience a change of mind so your life can go in a new direction.

How does this internal transformation take place? How can you live in such a way that you diminish the likelihood of falling back into addictive patterns? The next two chapters will answer these questions and help you devise a strategy for renewing your mind and find lasting freedom.

▼

CHAPTER 13

Finding the New You

I can't remember a time when I didn't think I was worse than just about everyone else. It's not that I lacked confidence in my abilities. Instead, I felt morally flawed.

I feared exposure. I feared if people ever saw the real me, they wouldn't like me. I assumed my destructive appetites would always control me. If I harnessed them for awhile, I felt it would just be a matter of time before they would break loose and run away with my life.

Since I viewed myself that way, I feared having children. After all, what if they were like me? What if they behaved like I did as a child?

It wasn't until my appetites had been under control for several years that I began to view myself differently. One day I was startled to realize my inner dragon had been asleep for a long time. My life seemed to be coming together. Even though I still struggled, I felt good about who I was and where I was headed.

How did it happen? Actually, it began with the realization that my dragon's power over me had been broken. Even today, when I find myself giving in to his spell, that truth gives me hope.

When I first realized that I was free from my powerful sinful nature, I felt like I had a magic wand. I thought I could wave it over my problems and—presto!—they'd vanish.

Such wasn't the case.

Though freedom begins by understanding that the dragon's power is broken, it only progresses as we apply what we've learned. Unfortunately, in the process of applying truth we often discover that our understanding is limited.

It reminds me of a story I heard about a banking executive who was retiring after a brilliant career. His success was legend. He had taken a small, struggling bank and built it into one of the strongest in the country.

The man replacing him was awed at the thought of stepping into his predecessor's shoes. Hoping to gain the inside track, the young man visited the retiring executive as he cleaned out his office.

"What's the secret of your success?" the young man asked.

"I made wise decisions," the executive replied. He dumped the contents of a drawer out on his desk and began untangling a web of rubber bands.

"Well, what's the key to making wise decisions?"

"Experience," the elderly gentleman said.

"And how do you get that?"

The older man smiled. "By making *bad* decisions!"

I chuckle every time I hear that story, because I carry scars from bad decisions that have given me experience. What you'll learn in this chapter will help you deal with your secret addictions. But the real help will occur as you gain experience by using what you've learned.

Paid in Full

Because shame is at the root of all addictions, it's crucial that you begin seeing yourself as God sees you. In Chapter 11

I gave you some suggestions for learning to love and accept yourself. I'd like to take those suggestions a step further.

God's unconditional acceptance is often difficult to comprehend. You may wonder how He can overlook all the terrible things you've done. Actually, He doesn't overlook them. On the contrary, Jesus died on a cross to pay for all the wrong things you've done.

When I first heard this message I was greatly relieved. While I was growing up my family seldom went to church. I wondered what a person had to do to be right with God.

I got all kinds of different answers from my religious friends. Some told me I had to go to church. Others said I had to stop swearing and be nice. Regardless of the formula, it seemed I had to win God's favor.

I realized that, if the only way to please God was by being religious and toeing the line, I was in deep trouble. I found church boring. I couldn't stop swearing. And I enjoyed the wild life.

I was thrilled when I discovered that all God asked me to do was trust His Son to forgive me. God only wanted me to believe that Jesus paid for my sins through His death and gave me life through His resurrection (Romans 4:5; 10:9-10; Ephesians 2:8-9). So one day I trusted Christ as my Savior.

What amazed me most were the immediate changes that occurred in my life. I shed habits I had struggled with for years. I was sure the dragon within had been put to sleep permanently.

Of course, it hadn't. And when the dragon stirred from its slumber after I had trusted Christ it scared me. That's when I found in the writings of Paul some insights that altered how I handled my addictive appetites. The more I learned, the more I wanted to live free of the dragon's terrorism. When I began to experience what the Bible calls walking in the light, I didn't want to return to the dragon's dark corner.

You're Not a Dragon, So
Don't Act Like One

When Paul wrote his letter to the church at Rome, he knew some would say his message of salvation by faith promotes lawlessness. They would argue that if God freely forgives all who believe in Christ, then nothing prevents people from satisfying their lower appetites.

Paul said such thinking fails to understand a spiritual reality. Namely, all who believe in Christ have died to the power of the dragon (Romans 6:1-14). He wrote, "We died to sin; how can we live in it any longer?" (v. 2). It's important to note that Paul didn't say our sin or dragon within died. He said *we* died.

Since none of us have died physically, Paul had to be referring to another kind of death. He taught that all who believe in Christ were identified with Him in His death, burial, and resurrection. It's not that we lose our individuality. Instead, we are indwelt by Christ. Everything that is true of Christ is true of us.

This concept has life-changing power, because it describes a spiritual reality. It describes the new you.

Does sin have power over Christ? Of course not! Paul wants us to realize it's inconsistent for us to allow the dragon to control our lives since we have died and been raised with Christ. We're new people, identified with Christ. The risen Lord of the universe actually lives in us!

Several years ago I heard a story about a sailor who served under a harsh and demanding captain. When he washed the deck, the captain would have him wash it again. When he painted the railings, the captain would have him add another coat.

Finally, the young sailor was discharged. No longer did he have to answer to the master who had controlled his every move.

Several weeks later, the young man ran into his old captain on the streets of the harbor town. When the captain saw him he gruffly ordered him to report back to the ship. The ex-sailor was so accustomed to obeying the captain's orders he immediately turned toward the wharf. Then he remembered he had been released from the captain's authority. He no longer had to obey him or even listen to him. Instead of returning to the ship, he shook his head and walked away a free man.

This story illustrates what Paul is teaching us in Romans 6. We've been released from the power of the sinful nature. It's inconsistent for us to obey its orders.

Count on It

Paul instructs us, "Count yourselves dead to sin" (v. 11). No longer are we to obey the dragon's commands or live under its authority. We possess victory in Christ and are to live in that victory.

The spiritual wealth we've acquired through Christ reminds me of the story of Raymond Krasky. For 20 years Krasky worked in the orchards of Oregon picking fruit. Finally he got a job on a ranch for $35 a week and a room. He cared for animals, mended fences, and worked with the irrigation system.

When Maynard Nelson found Krasky, the weather-beaten 61-year-old ranch hand was bent over, pulling wheels off a truck. Nelson was a private eye who specialized in finding people who have money coming to them.

"Are you Raymond Krasky?" Nelson asked. Krasky nodded. "I think I have some money you can claim." He sure did! Krasky had a $238,000 trust fund in an Oregon bank he never knew about.

Can you imagine how Krasky felt when he walked into that bank and made his first withdrawal? No longer did he have to live in poverty. He could count on his new-found wealth to change his life. Similarly, we can count on our position in Christ to change our lives.

What to Do When the Dragon Roars

The next time the dragon whispers in your ear about your addictive behavior, turn away from it and look to Christ. Don't struggle against the dragon yourself. Don't resist it by saying, "I can't listen to it." Instead turn to God and say, "Father, thank You for delivering me from my lower nature. Thank You for being my Dragonslayer."

If you try to fight the dragon, you'll lose. It's too powerful. Instead, allow God to fight your battle.

When I was in the ninth grade, Jack Hampton, a fellow student, despised me. Jack looked like a giant. He was a man among boys. He stood six feet three inches tall and weighed 230 pounds. I was only five feet nine inches tall and weighed 130 pounds. Jack's fist was almost as large as my head.

One night at a party Jack arrived late. When he discovered I was there, he hunted me down. In a few minutes he was calling me names and shoving me around. Like an idiot, I allowed him to coax me into the front yard where he said he was going to kill me.

I did everything short of falling on my knees and crying like a baby to talk Jack out of beating me up—and I would have done that if I thought it would work.

We were standing in the yard surrounded by about 30 kids who were urging me to hit Jack when a car screeched to a halt at the curb. A moment later the door slammed and someone yelled out, "Hampton!"

I recognized the voice. It was my best friend, Mike Temple. Mike was the only guy in town bigger and meaner than Jack Hampton. Before graduating from high school, Mike made the all-state football team twice as a fullback. Later he played college ball for Oklahoma State. He was a tough kid who loved to fight.

Mike quickly pushed his way through the crowd, walked up to Hampton, shoved him back, and said, "Hampton, if you're going to touch Perkins, you'll have to go through me."

I felt a surge of courage and stepped up to Jack. "That's right, Hampton," I said. "And don't forget it!"

Jack started whimpering about how he didn't realize Mike and I were buddies. He assured my friend he'd never bother me again.

I like that story because it illustrates how Jesus fights for me. I don't need to suffer any more humiliating defeats.

By faith we believe that Christ has delivered us from sin and our addiction. Our union with Him is the source of our self-control. We must accept with our spirits and minds the reality of His victory.

Saying Yes to God and No to the Dragon

But there's more to victory over our secret addictions than knowing where victory comes from. The battle against the dragon isn't won on the basis of understanding alone. Nor is victory assured simply because we have access to the power of God. Paul wrote, "Do not let sin reign in your mortal body so that you obey its evil desires. Do not offer the parts of your body to sin, as instruments of wickedness, but rather offer yourselves to God . . . and offer the parts of your body to him as instruments of righteousness" (Romans 6:12,13).

It takes time for sinful people to begin seeing themselves as God sees them. While the process is taking place, we must make choices about how we will use our minds and bodies. Both are instruments that the dragon and God want to use to accomplish their ends. The dragon will use your mind and body to feed on an addictive object or event. God will use you for His good and yours. Your responsibility is to look to God and hand your body over to Him for His purposes.

As you begin looking to God for victory over the dragon, your addictive appetites may hibernate for awhile. You may think an occasional experience with your addictive object or event is acceptable as long as you limit yourself. The thought may even occur to you that, since God has forgiven you completely, an occasional sin won't hurt.

Paul wrote, "Don't you know that when you offer yourselves to someone to obey him as slaves, you are slaves to the one whom you obey—whether you are slaves to sin, which leads to death, or to obedience, which leads to righteousness?" (Romans 6:16).

The point is clear. *You determine by your choices who will be your master.* If you give the dragon even a small snack, it will begin to take over your personality. I've spoken with food addicts who have controlled their eating for months. The dragon seemed absent. Then after a single binge he demanded more. The same thing is true no matter what your addiction.

On the other hand, if you give yourself to God, He will become your master.

Just because your lower nature is silent doesn't mean it's dead. It's dangerous to think, "I can feed it a little and it won't hurt." Feeding it a little may result in enslavement.

Three Steps to Victory

Before we move on, I'd like to summarize what we've learned in this chapter. There are three important elements that will help the new you experience victory over a secret addiction. It would be helpful for you to read these aloud until you've learned them. Once you have them memorized, repeat them aloud and often.

Perspective. I'm a new person. I see my dragon differently. I'm united with Christ, and the power of my sinful nature has been broken. I don't have to obey its commands any longer.

Presence. I'm not alone in my struggles. There is One beside me who knows my weakness and accepts me as I am, Jesus Christ the Dragonslayer.

Power. I have the power of the risen Christ living within me. I don't need to argue or fight with the dragon. I don't need to vow to resist its advances. When I am tempted, I can turn to Christ and utilize His power for victory.

Perspective, presence, and power are three ingredients that make up the new you. But finding freedom from your addiction requires another critical element. In the next chapter I'll help you see how you can stop acting out destructive behavior.

CHAPTER 14

Breaking the Addictive Cycle

During the conflict in the Falkland Islands between England and Argentina, the Royal Navy's 3,500-ton destroyer HMS Sheffield was sunk by a single missile fired from an Argentine fighter jet. It caused some people to wonder if modern surface warships were obsolete, sitting ducks for today's sophisticated missiles.

But a later discovery revealed that the Sheffield's defenses did pick up the incoming missile. The ship's computer correctly identified it as a French-made Exocet. But the computer was programmed to ignore Exocets as "friendly." The computer didn't recognize that the missile had been fired from an enemy plane. The ship was sunk by a missile it saw coming and could have evaded.

A similar thing happens to addicts. They allow enemy missiles to penetrate their defense systems because they don't identify them for what they are.

It would be nice if, once you devoted yourself to God, all danger disappeared. It doesn't work that way. Dedication to God and a determination to stop your addictive behavior are critical steps. But there is more to experiencing freedom from the dragon's traps. Finding freedom requires reprogramming your mind. It means developing an ability to identify and avoid dangerous situations.

This chapter will help you understand the addictive cycle and develop a personal strategy for breaking it.

The Addictive Cycle

As we've seen in previous chapters, we all have a dragon living in a corner of our heart. It's obsessed with gratification at any cost.

Your vows of commitment to God mean nothing to the dragon. At any moment it can roar out of its hiding place and overpower you, even when it appears to be asleep or dead.

It's important to realize that the dragon's emergence from the cave is part of a repeatable cycle. Earlier I noted the four stages of the addictive cycle: preoccupation, ritualization, acting out, and shame. I'd now like to look at these four stages from the perspective of James, the half-brother of Jesus, who wrote about the dangers of temptation.

It fascinates me that a man who wrote almost 2000 years ago so clearly defined the addictive cycle we struggle with today. The stages of temptation he mentions parallel the stages of the addictive cycle we've been discussing. James urged his readers to be aware of the process of temptation so they could avoid it.

1. Preoccupation—Enticement. James wrote, "Each one is tempted when, by his own evil desire, he is dragged away and enticed" (James 1:14). In the original language, the words for "dragged away" and "enticed" are fishing terms. They speak of a fish being drawn out of its hiding place and attracted by a tempting lure.

Expert fishermen know where big fish swim and how to catch them. Mark, a friend of mine, is such a fisherman. He has spent years locating the best fishing spots in the Pacific Northwest.

Early one morning my oldest son, Ryan, and I climbed into Mark's Bronco. Mark was going to show us how to catch the big ones. After driving a few hours we ended up by a river in the backwoods of Oregon. We hiked down a tree-lined trail to a rocky ledge overlooking a mountain stream.

"There are steelhead in there," Mark said, pointing to the deep, slow-moving water below us. "Bait your hooks the way I showed you and drop them in. You'll have a fish in no time."

Within a minute Ryan's rod bent down. His reel shrieked as a fish swam away with the hook. As Ryan pulled back on his rod, a three-foot steelhead arched out of the water. "Whoa, look at that!" he yelled.

Within an hour we had landed four fish. Ryan's weighed almost 20 pounds.

Mark's an expert fisherman who could earn a comfortable living as a fishing guide. He knows the right bait to drop in front of a fish to draw it out of hiding.

Unable to see the hook, the fish is captivated by the appeal of the bait. Even a grand-daddy fish, whose mouth is scarred from other hooks, is vulnerable to the right bait.

* He swims around the lure.

* He convinces himself there's no danger.

* He persuades himself he won't get caught.

* He believes he can take the bait and avoid the hook.

That's what happens in the first phase of the temptation cycle. The dragon of our own evil desire drops a lure in front of us. It whispers, "Looks good, doesn't it? It won't hurt to try it once more. You'll enjoy it. You deserve it."

With little resistance we listen to and believe the dragon's lies. We convince ourselves that we can play with the bait and not get hooked.

This is the stage of the cycle where you must take aggressive action. You need to catch yourself daydreaming about acting out your addiction. When you find yourself fantasizing, switch mental gears.

I urge people to memorize verses from the Bible to counteract destructive thoughts. I've found that memorizing large sections of the Bible gives me a safe mental focus when I'm tempted. By the time I recite a paragraph or two to myself, my spirit is strengthened and my mind is cleared.

The reason this works so well is because God uses the Bible to expose the danger of the bait. To a fish, bait looks like the real thing. It gives the illusion of real food. Similarly, the object or event of an addiction gives the illusion of intimacy. It promises to give us pleasure while filling the emptiness in our hearts. Meditating on the truth of Scripture helps us see the illusion for what it is.

There's another reason why meditating on Scripture helps disrupt the cycle. Our minds can only think about one thing at a time. As long as you're mentally reviewing Bible verses, your mind is distracted from the tempting thought or activity. If you have a close friend or support group, let them know you're struggling with preoccupation. Talking with a friend will help expose the illusion.

2. Ritualization—Conception. After describing the enticement stage of the cycle, James changed imagery. No longer did he use the terminology of a fisherman. Instead, he spoke of the birth process. He wrote, "After desire has conceived, it gives birth to sin" (v. 15). Minds enticed by evil desire become pregnant with sin.

At this stage addicts are fantasizing about the gratification acting out will provide. The seed of the act is present in our minds and growing. In fact, once the process reaches this stage, the act is virtually inevitable.

Like a pregnant woman buying baby clothes and nursery furniture, we anticipate an imminent delivery of the sinful act. While we haven't yet given birth to the deed, we're carrying out the rituals that precede it.

Nothing is more important for a person wanting to find freedom from addictive behavior than identifying the rituals that precede an episode of acting out.

- The food addict may have rituals that include shopping on an empty stomach or browsing through certain aisles at the supermarket.

- The sex addict may browse through a video store or cruise a neighborhood littered with prostitutes.

- The gambling addict may check the odds in the newspaper or visit a race track with the intention of only watching.

- A spending addict may go window shopping at a local mall.

- A helping addict may begin checking up on a family member's schedule.

Each of us has rituals unique to our addiction. Finding freedom means breaking the trance of the rituals. To do so, make a list of the rituals that lead up to your addictive behavior. Once the list is made, define what you must do to contain the rituals. Remember: Abstinence demands that you stop carrying out your rituals. You must be willing to take any steps necessary to keep yourself away from them. At this point there's no room for compromise. Holding onto even one ritual will nurture the dragon.

One woman who struggled with an eating addiction broke her ritual by taking a friend grocery shopping with her. Before they went to the store the woman explained to her friend how she could help by monitoring what she bought.

A shopping addict destroyed all her credit cards and made a list before shopping for clothes. She asked her husband to approve the list. Later she showed him what she bought.

A sex addict broke his ritual by removing cable television

from his home. As a further precaution he refused to watch television after 10 P.M. unless his wife was present.

These are examples of the kinds of aggressive steps that must be taken to contain an addiction.

As you make your list and prepare to break your ritual, the dragon will lean over your shoulder. It won't appear as the fire-breathing monster who's destroying your life. It'll seem harmless as a kitten. The dragon will plead with you to keep just one ritual—your favorite. It will promise never to ask for more.

You must anticipate the dragon's pleading and ignore it. Make your list and be ruthless. Identify every ritual that feeds the dragon.

3. Acting out—Birth. Birth naturally follows conception. The act that has been dreamed about and planned will be carried out. The tantalizing bait will be tasted. If addicts don't break the cycle at the enticement or conception stage, it's highly unlikely they will be able to prevent themselves from acting out their addictions.

- The food addict will binge.

- The sex addict will rent an X-rated video.

- The gambling addict will place his bet.

- The spending addict will make a big purchase.

- The helping addict will rescue his or her spouse.

4. Shame—Death. "Bill, I have a surprise," Cindy said. "We're going to have a baby!"

I'll never forget the excitement of anticipating the birth of our first child. Cindy and I made a list of things we'd need: crib, drapes, rocker, diapers, changing table, night light. What we didn't receive at baby showers we found at garage sales.

We took a class in natural childbirth. I liked my role of standing at Cindy's side reminding her to pant like a dog.

After nine months the big day arrived. At two in the morning on July 5th, 1976, we raced to the hospital. We had hoped for a natural birth, but after four or five hours the doctor concluded that the child would have to be delivered by Caesarean section.

I was standing by the nurse's station when I heard a baby crying on the speaker from the delivery room. Then I heard Cindy's voice: "Bill, God has given us a boy!" Later, I joined Cindy in the delivery room and marveled at my son's tiny hands and feet. What a day!

Before Ryan was born, Cindy and I occasionally talked about the possibility of something going wrong. How horrible it would be if our son was stillborn after all those months of preparation and dreaming. I can't imagine a pain deeper and more lingering than that caused by the death of a child.

But death always happens after we sin. James wrote, "Sin, when it is full-grown, gives birth to death" (v. 15). When an addict acts out, the outcome is always pain and shame.

The dragon always promises life, joy, and intimacy from the addictive behavior. During the period of enticement, conception, and birth, these promises appear valid. But they're not. The "child" is always stillborn.

- Instead of life, the dragon gives death.

- Instead of joy, the dragon gives shame.

- Instead of intimacy, the dragon gives an illusion.

Addictive behavior always leads to despair.

Ask King David. After his illicit affair with Bathsheba, he murdered her husband, Uriah. Later, the child which resulted from the affair died.

Ask Samson. After his affair with Delilah he lost his sight and sacrificed his place of leadership.

Ask the men and women whose names appear in the newspapers every week, those who sacrificed their families or reputations while feeding an addiction.

But go further. Have you ever acted out your addiction and escaped the consequences? Perhaps for awhile. But eventually you experienced the loss. Nobody escapes the consequences of their addictions—nobody! When we act out we pay a high price.

But we don't have to act out. We can contain the dragon and move forward with our lives by breaking the cycle at its earliest stages.

Find a Friend

The exercises I've suggested in this chapter and the next will help you contain and cut off your addiction. They are critical steps you must take to experience freedom.

But you'll need a friend to help you take these steps. In selecting a helper, find someone who accepts you as you are, someone with whom you aren't afraid to be vulnerable.

For example, I meet with a small group of men every week. One of the prerequisites for being a part of our group is an admission of need. We openly talk about our lives. We share our struggles and failures. We develop personal strategies for keeping ourselves under control. During periods of vulnerability to temptation we faithfully phone one another to receive additional support.

Our group has agreed that we will only speak the truth to one another. We discuss rituals we must avoid and challenge one another to ruthlessly deal with dangerous preoccupations. We continually remind each other, "By the grace of God, you can do it!"

Comforted to Comfort·

It would be easy for someone who struggles with an addiction to wonder what good can come from such a struggle. I understand. I look back on segments of my life with genuine regret. At times I wish I could clip them from my memory like segments of a videotape.

But I realize that my experiences of struggle and failure have deepened my dependence on God. They have also helped me understand the suffering other people experience from an addiction. Paul wrote, "Praise be to the God and Father of our Lord Jesus Christ, the Father of compassion and the God of all comfort, who comforts us in all our troubles, so that we can comfort those in any trouble with the comfort we ourselves have received from God" (2 Corinthians 1:3,4).

I thank God that He accepts us as we are through His Son. He sees our failures and loves us anyway. But He does more. He wraps us in the blanket of His comfort and heals our hurts. Then He enables us to offer that same blanket of comfort and healing to others.

▼

CHAPTER 15

Tools
for Tight
Corners

As I snapped the fitting onto the end of the socket wrench, I figured it would be an easy job. It shouldn't take more than 30 minutes at the most. I'd take out the old kitchen faucet and put in the new one. No sweat!

The job would have been easy too, except for one thing: My wrench wouldn't fit through the tiny space between the back of the sink and the wall. For over an hour I pushed, pulled, twisted, and pried. I tried every conceivable angle. But I couldn't get the end of the wrench over the head of the nut.

I was about to give up when I thought of my neighbor. Ernie collects tools. He has more tools he's never used than I have tools. He says he likes to have them so they'll be there when he needs them.

When I told him about my struggle, he smiled. "I have a set of plumber's tools made exactly for that job." He handed me the set of wrench extensions. "You'll be the first to use them."

I took the extensions home, and three minutes later I had the first nut off. An impossible job had become a breeze. The right tool solved the problem created by a tight corner.

As you move forward with your life of freedom from addiction, you will face difficult tight corners. Temptations, disappointments, or relapses will cause you to fear you're not going to make it. At such times you'll feel like raising the white flag.

Don't do it! Instead, pull out a tool that will help you solve the problem and continue on. This chapter is a tool box filled with tools you can use when you're in a tight corner and to help keep you out of them. Read it carefully so you know where each tool is and how to use it. Mark those tools you may need first so you'll be able to get to them quickly.

A Calendar

A calendar will serve you well. With this tool you can monitor your progress.

To abstain from your addiction you must live one day at a time. Don't think about quitting for a week, month, or year. Instead, begin every day with a fresh commitment to avoid feeding the dragon for 24 hours. At the end of each day, mark your calendar for another successful day completed.

If you relapse, indicate on your calendar exactly what triggered your fall. Over time you'll likely see a pattern of temptation emerging for particular times of the week or month. You'll also begin to identify the kinds of situations that entice you.

Once you see the rhythm of your life recorded on your calendar, you'll be able to anticipate times of vulnerability and cope with them more effectively.

A Safety Guard Against Rituals

A good power saw has a safety guard to protect your hands and allow you to cut wood without cutting off a finger. In overcoming your addictive behavior, you need to put safety guards in place. It's crucial for you to identify the circumstances, conversations, and relationships that prompt you to act out your addiction. All trigger objects or events must have a safety guard around them.

You can construct such a shield by identifying the rituals that trigger your addictive behavior and removing them from your life. Use the following format to build a guard over your rituals.

Rituals that Trigger My Addiction	How I Will Avoid Them
1.	
2.	
3.	
4.	
5.	
6.	

Healthy Self-Talk

Since the dragon wants to fill your mind with feelings of shame and self-hatred, you need to counteract its tactics with healthy, Scripture-based self-talk. Repeat the following phrase aloud throughout the day: *God unconditionally loves me, and I receive His love and accept myself.*

The more you say it, the sooner you'll believe it. The sooner you believe it, the sooner you'll act like it's true.

A Support Team

If God intended for you to live alone He would have put you on a private island. But He didn't. He intends for us to care for and support each other as we find freedom from our addictions.

True intimacy is an addiction's greatest enemy. You need a friend who will love and accept you, pray for you, and speak the truth to you.

As you meet with this special friend, several guidelines are crucial:

- You must both admit you have needs that you can't meet alone.

- You must both agree to always speak the truth in love.

- You must both agree to meet regularly.

After you've been meeting for awhile, you may want to add another friend or, at the most, two.

The first step in overcoming an addiction is admitting to your support team your helplessness and the seriousness of your problem. Once you admit that your life is out of control, you're on the way to freedom.

But remember: The dragon isn't dead. It will try to pull you into a mind-set of denial even after you've admitted your struggle to your friends. When you find yourself falling back into that trap, don't clam up. Whenever you deny your struggle you're withdrawing from God and those who love you.

It's crucial that you speak openly with your support team about your struggles and failures. They need to understand your rituals and encourage you to avoid them. Honesty is the antidote for denial.

Experience has taught me that I grow fastest in a garden with other growing plants. Don't try to make it alone. Be accountable to someone.

Patient Hope

Don't be surprised if, after a few days or weeks of abstinence, the dragon comes roaring out of its cave. Addictions are deep-rooted problems, and they take a long time to heal. The words of Isaiah offer encouragement: "Those who hope in the Lord will renew their strength. They will soar on wings like eagles; they will run and not grow weary, they will walk and not be faint" (Isaiah 40:31).

Pain

As you grow in your freedom from addiction, it's important to remember that pain isn't your enemy. Pain is a tool that will make you stronger. Don't run away from it or try to anesthetize it. Remember: You became addicted when you tried to anesthetize your pain. Eventually, that which deadened the pain created more suffering than it eliminated.

Instead of running from pain, ride it out like you would a rising tide. Eventually it will recede.

Nobody passes through life without hardship. Even the apostle Paul experienced intense pain when he was afflicted with a thorn in the flesh (2 Corinthians 12:7-9). While we don't know for sure the source of Paul's pain, we know he suffered greatly. Three times he begged God to take it away. Three times God refused. Instead of removing the cause of his suffering, God gave Paul an extra measure of His grace.

Rather than becoming angry with God, Paul wrote, "I will boast all the more gladly about my weaknesses, so that Christ's power may rest on me. That is why, for Christ's sake, I delight in weaknesses, in insults, in hardships, in persecutions, in difficulties. For when I am weak, then I am strong" (vv. 9,10).

Paul learned how to rely on the grace of God during his times of suffering. While the pain wasn't removed, he experienced the strength needed to endure with dignity.

Thankfully, that same grace is available to you. When you hurt, ask God to give you the grace you need to endure. Ask Him to make His strength apparent through your weakness.

A Consequences and Benefits List

Usually the pleasure of acting out is limited to a few minutes or hours, but the consequences may last a lifetime. Many people who were once addicted have found that comparing the consequences of addiction with the benefits of abstinence helps them avoid acting out. Periodically turn to Chapter 13 in this book and complete the exercise outlined there for these two lists.

Tears

Tears are tools to help us heal. I recently read that tears are the body's way of washing away toxic chemicals. Tears clean the soul and the body. When we hold them back we dam up an emotional stream that needs to flow for the heart to stay pure.

Even Jesus cried. When his friends Martha and Mary wept over the death of their brother, Lazarus, Jesus wept too. His rough carpenter's hands wiped the tears from his cheeks.

As you review the hurt you've suffered, you may need to cry. Disappointment may have taken a toll. The abuse still hurts.

Go ahead and weep. It's okay. Grieve over your disappointments and losses. God understands. As you cry, imagine Him wrapping His arms around you. God loves you and desires to heal your hurts.

Forgiveness

Forgiveness is an invaluable tool for finding freedom and healing from your addiction. There are three dimensions of forgiveness you need to employ.

Finding forgiveness. No matter what you may have done, God offers you forgiveness. Regardless of how terrible your shame and torturous your guilt, forgiveness is yours for the taking.

The Bible is filled with stories of people who fell and then found forgiveness.

- With Moses it was murder.

- With Rahab it was prostitution.

- With David it was adultery and murder.

- With Peter it was denying he knew the Lord.

All of these people and more found God eager to forgive their sins.

There is no need for you to continue to punish yourself for past wrongs. Jesus died on the cross and was punished in your place. He took upon Himself all of your wrongdoing and suffered the punishment you deserved (2 Corinthians 5:21; Romans 5:8). Three days later He rose from the dead, leaving your guilt and shame forever buried.

His forgiveness is available. Simply express to Him your desire to accept Him and His forgiveness (John 3:16). Once you've been forgiven by God, there's no need to condemn yourself. When you hear voices of self-condemnation, say to yourself: God forgives me and I forgive myself.

Extending forgiveness. As God has forgiven you, so you must forgive those who hurt you. That's not easy, especially if your wounds are deep and festering. But healing requires cleaning them out by forgiving those who hurt you.

"But I can't," you might say. "You don't understand what they've done to me."

You're right, I don't. I'm sorry you've been hurt. But you've certainly not been brutalized more than Jesus was when the Romans nailed Him to the cross. Yet God's Son extended His forgiveness to those who killed Him (Luke 23:24).

"But, I'm not God," you may argue.

I realize that. But if you'll turn to God, He will give you the strength you need to forgive.

There is a difference between forgiveness and reconciliation. Reconciliation can only occur when the offending person realizes the depth of hurt they've caused and seeks forgiveness. Even when reconciliation doesn't occur, you still need to forgive. You may forgive someone and never be reconciled with them.

Once you've told God you forgive the one who hurt you, each time you remember the hurt, pray for that person. Prayer is a great antidote for bitterness and wrath.

Seeking forgiveness. It may be that you have hurt others in the course of your addiction. As you reflect on your past, people you've hurt may come to mind. You may need to seek forgiveness from those people.

Before you get in touch with them, think through what you'll say. Avoid blaming them for your actions. Nobody wants to hear someone who's hurt them say something like, "After you lied and cheated me out of my money, I became angry and said some unkind words. Will you forgive me?"

Be honest and get straight to the point. When I go to those I've hurt, I say something like this: "I now see that I've wronged you by (my offense) . I'm deeply sorry. Will you forgive me?" I suggest you use a similar approach.

I encourage people to make these contacts in person or over the phone. Writing out your request for forgiveness isn't a good idea unless it's the only way to communicate with the person. A letter could fall into the wrong hands and cause greater pain.

Wounded persons are sometimes suspicious of attempts at reconciliation. They may even withhold forgiveness. Don't argue with them or try to persuade them. Tell them you understand, and request their prayers. If they pray for you, the time may come when they'll forgive you.

It's important to realize that people who forgive you are not obligated to renew a relationship with you. You're not seeking a total restoration of the relationship. You're simply seeking forgiveness. If something more occurs, that's great. But be careful not to place expectations on the persons from whom you seek forgiveness.

Bible Meditation

Nothing has facilitated my own freedom from addiction like memorizing and meditating on Bible verses that address my needs. Just as an addiction destroys the real you, meditation on Scripture nurtures the real you.

The following passages have proven helpful to me. Whenever I am discouraged or tempted, I review them and gain direction and strength.

Temptation. "No temptation has seized you except what is common to man. And God is faithful; he will not let you be tempted beyond what you can bear. But when you are tempted, he will also provide a way out so that you can stand up under it" (1 Corinthians 10:13).

"Blessed is the man who perseveres under trial, because when he has stood the test, he will receive the crown of life that God has promised to those who love him. When tempted, no one should say, 'God is tempting me.' For God cannot be tempted by evil, nor does he tempt anyone; but each one is tempted when, by his own evil desire, he is dragged away and enticed. Then, after desire has conceived, it gives birth to sin; and sin, when it is full-grown, gives birth to death" (James 1:12-15).

Anxiety. "Do not be anxious about anything, but in everything, by prayer and petition, with thanksgiving, present your requests to God. And the peace of God, which transcends all understanding, will guard your hearts and your minds in Christ Jesus" (Philippians 4:6,7).

"But seek first his kingdom and his righteousness, and all these things will be given to you as well" (Matthew 6:33).

Negativism. "Finally, brothers, whatever is true, whatever is noble, whatever is right, whatever is pure, whatever is lovely, whatever is admirable—if anything is excellent or praiseworthy—think about such things" (Philippians 4:8).

"Give thanks in all circumstances, for this is God's will for you in Christ Jesus" (1 Thessalonians 5:18).

Lust. "Flee from sexual immorality. All other sins a man commits are outside his body, but he who sins sexually sins against his own body" (1 Corinthians 6:18).

Contentment. "Keep your lives free from the love of money and be content with what you have, because God has said, 'Never will I leave you; never will I forsake you'" (Hebrews 13:5).

Forgiveness. "Then Peter came to Jesus and asked, 'Lord, how many times shall I forgive my brother when he sins against me? Up to seven times?' Jesus answered, 'I tell you, not seven times, but seventy-seven times'" (Matthew 18:21, 22).

"If we confess our sins, he is faithful and just and will forgive us our sins and purify us from all unrighteousness" (1 John 1:9).

"Blessed is he whose transgressions are forgiven, whose sins are covered" (Psalms 32:1).

Prayer. "The Lord is near to all who call on him, to all who call on him in truth" (Psalms 145:18).

"Ask and it will be given to you; seek and you will find; knock and the door will be opened to you. For everyone who asks receives; he who seeks finds; and to him who knocks, the door will be opened" (Matthew 7:7,8).

Self-image. "Therefore, if anyone is in Christ, he is a new creation; the old has gone, the new has come!" (2 Corinthians 5:17).

"For you created my inmost being; you knit me together in my mother's womb. I praise you because I am fearfully and wonderfully made; your works are wonderful, I know that full well" (Psalm 139:13,14).

"I have been crucified with Christ and I no longer live, but Christ lives in me. The life I live in the body, I live by faith in the Son of God, who loved me and gave himself for me" (Galatians 2:20).

"Since, then, you have been raised with Christ, set your hearts on things above, where Christ is seated at the right hand of God. Set your minds on things above, not on earthly things. For you died, and your life is now hidden with Christ in God" (Colossians 3:1-3).

Fasting

I mention fasting with hesitancy. For those of you with eating addictions, the risks of fasting may be so great you should avoid it.

Fasting isn't something done to lose weight or purge the body and spirit. It's a means of focusing the mind and spirit on God and nurturing your inner person.

Fasting softens my heart toward God and other people more than any other spiritual discipline (Isaiah 55:2-11). It teaches me to say no to my appetite for food, which strengthens my will in other areas.

When you fast try to take time for an extended period of Bible reading and prayer. Ask the Lord to soften your heart and give you new direction.

If you're considering a fast, consult your physician and

tell him of your plans. Make sure you get his approval along with any suggestions he may have for this discipline.

Prayer

Prayer is talking with God. It involves telling Him about your problems, joys, and needs as well as those of your loved ones.

Prayer is the way you stay connected to the One who gives you His love and acceptance along with the power you need to overcome your dragon.

But your prayers don't obligate God to give you what you request. Just as a father sometimes says no to a child, so God may say no to you. His denial of a request doesn't show a lack of love. All of His actions are motivated by love.

If prayer isn't something you've ever scheduled, I'd encourage you to pray while you drive. Turn off your radio and carry on a conversation with God. Do it aloud. Once you develop that habit, try to carve out a time slot each day when you can get alone with God and pray.

Journaling

Each day I try to write in my journal. For me this doesn't mean writing pages of poetry. It involves recording the key events of my day and my spiritual temperature. I also try to write out a prayer or two so I'll have something to refer back to when the prayers are answered.

Keeping a journal is a tangible way of nurturing your spiritual self. Remember: An addiction destroys your inner self. Bible meditation, fasting, journaling, and prayer strengthen your spirit by helping you develop intimacy with God.

Relapse

I wish I could guarantee that you'll never relapse into

your addiction. I can't. But if you fall, don't give up seeking your freedom.

You may tend to think, "Now that I've blown it, I might as well quit trying." You must avoid such destructive thinking! If you relapse, rebound. You're not starting all over. Focus on the fact that you went for awhile without acting out. Allow your disappointment to be a reminder of your vulnerability and need to depend on God. Let it be a reminder of the situations you need to avoid in the future.

God has forgiven you. You must accept His forgiveness and move on. If the Lord of the universe has forgiven you, you don't need to wallow in self-condemnation.

Intimacy

I can't overstate the importance of an intimate relationship with God. Because the object or event to which we become addicted gives the *illusion* of intimacy, only *authentic* intimacy can expose the illusion.

God doesn't simply want us to experience freedom from our addictions, He wants us to enjoy Him. He calls us to an intimate relationship with Himself.

The night before His death, as Jesus walked to Gethsemane with His disciples, He recognized a plant growing in a field beside the road. For thousands of years that type of plant had grown on the earth. Now the Lord would use it to illustrate the relationship He desired between Himself and His disciples.

Jesus said He was the "true vine." He was the reality which the grapevine illustrated (John 15:1). Only by being connected to Jesus through faith, as a branch is connected to a vine, can we draw life from God.

The Lord also noted that only those branches which remain in Him will bear fruit. Remaining in Christ speaks of maintaining an unbroken connection. It refers to the necessity of our cultivating an intimate relationship with Christ so that we draw our life and strength from Him—just as a branch does from a vine.

But how do we remain or abide in the Lord? Jesus indicted that prayer and meditation upon His Word are two crucial ways (John 15:7) Earlier I mentioned that prayer and Bible meditation strengthen your relationship with God. When you pray you talk with God. When you read the Bible you're listening to God. As you remain in Christ, He will enable you to obey Him and experience His abiding joy (John 15:11).

As long as a branch remains attached to a healthy vine, it will bear fruit. The same is true of us. God doesn't simply command us to be fruitful. He produces in us the fruit which He wants us to bear. I think it's fascinating that Jesus used the word "remain" or "abide" ten times in seven verses (John 15:4-10). He knew that the key to our becoming all God wants us to be is our relationship with Him.

Every spring I prune the trees in my yard. Once a branch is separated from the tree, its leaves shrivel up and die. The same is true of us. Apart from an intimate relationship with God our spirits become barren.

God calls us to Himself, not just so we can be free of destructive addictions but so we can enjoy Him. As we grow in our relationship with Him, the illusion of intimacy provided by our addictions will become less appealing.

Such knowledge is a powerful tool. You can put it to use by thinking about God throughout the day. Replace a preoccupation with your addiction with thoughts about God. Talk with Him. When you're in battle, consciously draw on His strength. When you're content, give Him thanks. View your time of healing as a season to become more intimate with God... that's what He's waiting for.

A Final Thought

You're on the last lines of a book written to help you overcome a fatal attraction. I wish the two of us could talk about what you've learned. Of course, we can't. Books are like that.

But before we part, I want you to take a final look at the cave in the corner of your soul, the one where the dragon lives.

Don't fear it. Don't run from it. And don't worry about how you'll fight it. God sees into the dragon's lair. He understands its tactics. And God is on your side.

Remember that.

▼

Appendices

Notes

▲

▼

Masturbation

One evening, after I had spoken on the subject of sexual addictions, a middle-aged man said he needed to talk with me privately. After we were comfortably seated at a table, he asked, "Bill, is masturbation wrong?"

On another occasion, a woman in her mid-twenties told me, "Don't think that men are the only ones who struggle with masturbation. They aren't!"

After the publication of *Fatal Attractions* in the fall of '91, I realized I had failed to address an important issue. It's common knowledge that a high percentage of men acknowledge that they have masturbated in the past. Others admit they presently masturbate. And recent surveys indicate an increasingly large number of women acknowledge they practice this sexual behavior.

While many people admit that they masturbate, most are a bit uncertain concerning the moral implications of the practice. That's probably why I'm frequently asked, "Is masturbation wrong?" or "Is masturbation a destructive habit or addiction?"

Those questions would be easier to answer if the Bible provided a definitive statement on the subject. But it doesn't.

As is often the case, when God doesn't specifically address an issue, people have developed differing views.

For instance, David Wilkerson, in his book, *This Is Loving?* says, "Masturbation is not a gift of God for sex drives. Masturbation is not moral behavior and is not condoned in the Scriptures.... Masturbation is not harmless fun" (David Wilkerson, *This Is Loving?* Ventura, CA: Gospel Light, 1972, p. 40; as quoted by Jim Burns in *Radical Respect*, Eugene, OR: Harvest House, 1991, p. 158). On the other hand, Charlie Shedd, a respected Christian authority on sex and dating, calls masturbation a "gift of God" (Charlie Shedd, *The Stork Is Dead*, Waco, TX: Word Book Publishers, 1968, p. 83; as quoted by Jim Burns in *Radical Respect*, p. 159).

Some who believe masturbation is wrong try to prove their point by referring to the Old Testament character, Onan. After the death of Onan's brother, he had a responsibility to produce offspring with his brother's widow, Tamar (Genesis 38:8-10; Deuteronomy 25:5,6). Apparently Onan wanted to have sex with Tamar but he didn't want to bear children. To keep her from getting pregnant, "Whenever he lay with his brother's wife, he spilled his semen on the ground" (Genesis 38:9). Onan's behavior so displeased the Lord that He took Onan's life (v. 10).

Even a casual look at this passage reveals that it has nothing to do with masturbation. God didn't condemn Onan for masturbating. He punished him for using Tamar to satisfy his sexual desire without fulfilling his responsibility to his dead brother.

When Is Masturbation Wrong?

My personal opinion is that masturbation is amoral. Under some circumstances it is acceptable behavior. On other occasions it is clearly wrong. As I've examined the Scriptures I've observed three guidelines aimed at helping a person determine whether or not their behavior is destructive.

The thought test. In Matthew 5:28 Jesus said, "Anyone who looks at a woman lustfully has already committed adultery with her in his heart." While the act of masturbation may not be wrong, fantasizing about having sex with someone other than your marriage partner is clearly wrong. The words of Jesus would certainly indicate that masturbation accompanied by the reading of pornographic literature or the viewing of pornographic videos is wrong. Again, the wrong isn't in the act of masturbation, it's in the accompanying thoughts.

The test of self-control. Masturbation which is obsessive-compulsive is also destructive. Several years ago a young man told me that he masturbated three or four times a day. His entire life revolved around when and where he would masturbate. While his case is an extreme example, there are others who find they can't resist the urge to masturbate. In 1 Corinthians 6:12, Paul wrote, " 'Everything is permissible for me'—but not everything is beneficial. 'Everything is permissible for me'—but I will not be mastered by anything." While masturbation may not be wrong, it is wrong for our lives to be controlled by habitual or addictive masturbation.

Obsessive-compulsive masturbation is often accompanied by behavior which is both demeaning and destructive. It tends to occur in an atmosphere lacking in intimacy and genuine caring. The chapter on sexual addictions sheds considerable light on this particular behavior.

The test of love. During a counseling session, a young woman blurted out, "Bill, Shawn never wants to have sex with me anymore. When we first got married that was all he wanted to do. Now, we only have sex once a month and that's when I beg him."

After meeting alone with Shawn, he told me, "It's just easier to read pornography and masturbate. I've done that for years. It saves me the hassle of dealing with my wife."

I wish I could say such behavior is rare. It isn't. Men and women who want sexual gratification without intimacy and self-sacrifice will often masturbate. Obviously, when masturbation drains a person of sexual energy, their spouse will suffer the consequences.

Paul addressed this issue in 1 Corinthians 7:3-5 when he wrote, "The husband should fulfill his marital duty to his wife, and likewise the wife to her husband. The wife's body does not belong to her alone but also to her husband. In the same way, the husband's body does not belong to him alone but also to his wife. Do not deprive each other except by mutual consent and for a time, so that you may devote yourselves to prayer. Then come together again so that Satan will not tempt you because of your lack of self-control."

Many people misinterpret Paul's words to mean that a husband or wife has a right to demand that their spouse sexually satisfy them. That's not what Paul said! In fact, he said just the opposite. He stated that neither the husband or wife is to demand from their spouse. Instead, they are to offer everything. Paul's focus was on giving not taking.

A loving husband will say to himself, "My body belongs to my wife. How can I use it to satisfy her?" Likewise, a loving wife will say, "My body belongs to my husband. How can I use it to satisfy him?" The husband or wife who masturbates, and in doing so deprives their spouse, isn't acting with love.

But what is a loving husband or wife to do if their sexual appetite is double that of their spouse? They could allow their spouse to satisfy them. They could abstain and use the sexual energy to express affection in non-sexual ways. They could masturbate at a time that wouldn't prevent them from meeting their partner's sexual needs.

When Is Masturbation Acceptable?

Obviously, there are as many unique situations as there are unique individuals. It would be impossible and foolish of me to try to walk through each situation. I believe the three tests I've mentioned provide a guideline which can be applied to most situations.

Whether you're married or single, ask yourself: 1. Does my behavior involve impure thoughts? 2. Am I in control of my behavior or am I controlled by my behavior? 3. Is my behavior preventing me from meeting my spouse's sexual needs?

Ultimately, each of us has to determine before God whether our attitudes and actions are pleasing to Him.

▼

Support Groups and Other Sources of Help

Now that you've read this book, if you feel that you need immediate help, please call:

New Life Treatment Center
1-800-332-TEEN (for adolescents)
1-800-277-LIFE (for adult treatment)
Stephen Arterburn, Founder and Chairman

These resources for healing and freedom from addictions can provide you with additional help. The support groups will welcome you without prejudice and make available to you other information suited to your specific needs. Note: Some of these resources have a Christian base but many do not.

Local chapters of these groups can be reached by consulting the white pages of your phone directory. If you can't locate what you need, call a related group for help or search the phone book of a larger city nearby.

The people who make up these groups are individuals much like yourself. They come together to strengthen one another and provide assistance to people with struggles like their own.

Support Groups

Alcoholics Anonymous
P.O. Box 459
Grand Central Station
New York, NY 10163
(212) 686-1100

Al-Anon/Alateen Family
   Group Headquarters, Inc.
P.O. Box 182
Madison Square Station
New York, NY 10159
1-800-356-9996

Debtors Anonymous
314 W. 53rd St.
New York, NY 10019
(212) 969-0710

National Association for
   Children of Alcoholics
31582 Coast Highway,
   Suite B
South Laguna, CA 92677
(714) 499-3889

Incest Survivors Anonymous
P.O. Box 5613
Long Beach, CA 90800

Overcomers Outreach
2290 W. Whittier Blvd.,
   Suite D
La Habra, CA 90631
(213) 697-3994

Overeaters Anonymous,
   World Services Office
2190 190th St.
Torrence, CA 90504

Gamblers Anonymous
P.O. Box 17173
Los Angeles, CA 90017
(213) 386-8789

Narcotics Anonymous
World Service Office
16155 Wyandotte St.
Van Nuys, CA 91406
(818) 780-3951

Codependents Anonymous
P.O. Box 33577
Phoenix, AZ 85087-3577
(602) 944-0141

Emotions Anonymous
P.O. Box 4245
St. Paul, MN 55104
(612) 647-9712

National Clearinghouse for
   Alcohol Information
P.O. Box 1908
Rockville, MD 20850

Adult Children of Alcoholics
   Central Service Board
P.O. Box 35623
Los Angeles, CA 90035
(213) 464-4423

(Alcoholics and adult
children of alcoholics
claiming Christ's promises
and accepting His healing)

Organizations

The following organizations may be listed in your local
phone book.

Adult Children of Alcoholics Anonymous
Al-Atot
Alcoholics Victorious (Christian Recovery
    support group)
Bulemic/Anorexics Anonymous
Child Abusers Anonymous
Cocaine Anonymous
Codependents of Sex Addicts
Parents Anonymous
Pills Anonymous
Sexaholics Anonymous
Sex and Love Addicts Anonymous
Shoplifters Anonymous
Smokers Anonymous
Spenders Anonymous
Victims of Incest Can Emerge
Workaholics Anonymous

Notes

Chapter 1
1. Melody Beattie, *Codependent No More* (San Francisco: Harper and Row, 1987), adapted from p. 7.
2. Ibid., p. 31.

Chapter 2
1. Gerald G. May, M.D., *Addiction and Grace* (San Francisco: Harper and Row, 1988), pp. 24-25.
2. Lawrence J. Hatterer, *The Pleasure Addicts* (New York: A.S. Barnes and Co., 1980), p. 17.
3. Craig Nakken, *The Addictive Personality* (New York: Harper and Row, 1988), p. 5.
4. Ibid., p. 7.
5. Archibald D. Hart, *Healing Life's Hidden Addictions* (Ann Arbor, MI: Servant Publications, 1990), p. 3.

Chapter 3
1. Abraham Twerski, *Addictive Thinking* (San Francisco: Harper and Row, 1990), p. 5.
2. Ibid., p. 10.
3. Ibid., p. 61.
4. Erich Fromm, *Sane Society* (New York: Fawcett, 1977).
5. Nakken, *The Addictive Personality*, p. 40.
6. In his book, *The Addictive Personality*, Dr. Nakken provides an extended discussion of the stages of addiction. I'm indebted to him for many of his insights.

Chapter 4
1. Dan B. Allender, *The Wounded Heart* (Colorado Springs, CO: NavPress, 1990), p. 46.
2. Frank Minirth, Paul Meier, Robert Hemfelt, and Sharon Sneed, *Love Hunger* (Nashville, TN: Thomas Nelson Publishers, 1990), pp. 13-14.
3. Ibid., p. 32.

Chapter 5

1. *People Weekly*, March 7, 1988, pp. 38-39.
2. Patrick Carnes, *Out of the Shadows* (Minneapolis, MN: CompCare Publications, 1893), p. 10.
3. H. Eist and A. Mandel, "Family Treatment of On-going Incest Behavior," *Family Process*, 1968, 7:216.
4. Roger Hillerstrom, *Intimate Deception* (Portland, OR: Multnomah Press, 1989), p. 113.
5. Carnes, *Out of the Shadows*, p. 27.
6. Nakken, *The Addictive Personality*, p. 24.
7. Carnes, *Out of the Shadows*, p. 160.

Chapter 6

1. Beattie, *Codependent No More*, p. 31.
2. John Bradshaw, *Bradshaw on the Family* (Deerfield Beach, IL: Health Communications, 1988), pp. 163-164.
3. Ibid., p. 165.
4. Claude M. Steiner, *Scripts People Live* (New York: Grove Press, 1974).

Chapter 7

1. Cliff Pfenning, "Lonely, Exhilarating Surfer's Life," *The Eugene Register-Guard*, March 12, 1991.
2. Hart, *Healing Life's Hidden Addictions*, p. 171.
3. Ibid., p. 172.
4. Richard Benyo, *The Exercise Fix* (Champaign, IL: Leisure Press, 1990), p. 84.
5. Ibid., p. 92.
6. Ibid., p. 68.
7. Ibid., pp. 14-15.
8. Ibid., p. 4.
9. Ibid., pp. 99-100.

Chapter 8

1. Hart, *Healing Life's Hidden Addictions*, p. 3.
2. Ibid., p. 8.
3. Ibid., p. 9.
4. Cherie Carter-Scott, *Negaholics* (New York: Villard Books, 1989), p. 85.
5. Ibid., pp. 60-65.

Chapter 9
1. Diane Fassel, *Working Ourselves to Death* (New York: Harper Collins Publishers, 1990), p. 2.
2. Christian Barnard and Curtis Bill Pepper, *One Life* (Toronto, Ontario: The MacMillan Company, 1969), p. 253.
3. Fassel, *Working Ourselves to Death*, pp. 29-30.

Chapter 11
1. Dr. Paul Brand and Philip Yancey, *In His Image* (Grand Rapids, MI: Zondervan Publishers, 1984), pp. 25-29.

Chapter 13
1. Twersky, *Addictive Thinking*, pp. 79-80.
2. Ibid., p. 82.
3. Tim Timmons, *Anybody Anonymous* (Old Tappan, NJ: Fleming H. Revell, 1990), pp. 49-50.

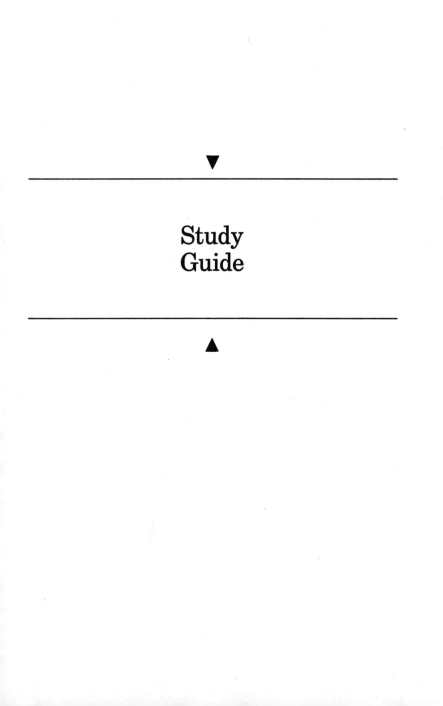

▼

Study
Guide

▲

1-2
Why Do Bad Things Look So Good?

I've always been fascinated by things that are off-limits. Early in my life I noticed that some of the things I *shouldn't* do often looked better to me than things I *should* do. And later in life I began to understand why. I realized that bad things look good because they offer a quick fix to painful feelings. Often, the relief and pleasure they offer seem too great to turn down. And, as if this weren't enough of a pull, evil spiritual forces in the universe have the power to give these forbidden things a glitter that attracts. Despite that fact, you and I can overcome the attraction of the bad. We can effectively resist the bad things which look so good.

A Closer Look at *Fatal Attractions* (p. 26)

I define an addict as a person who is unable to resist the repeated urge to enter into a love relationship with an object or event for the pleasure and illusion of intimacy it provides.

1. Reread the definitions of an addiction on pages 25 and 26. Which of the less technical definitions do you most identify with?

Now write your own definition of addiction:

I compare an addiction to an idol (p. 27):

An idol can be any object of extreme devotion, and idolatry is the activity of attaching ourselves to and worshiping that object. The more I understand about addiction, the more I'm convinced it is a deep-seated form of idolatry. The danger we face when we become idolaters is cutting ourselves off from God and others. No wonder idolatry is among those things God expressly forbids (Galatians 5:19-21).

2. How do you think obsessions with an object or event begin? How do they come to take the place of God in our lives? Give an example from your own observations of life.

A Closer Look at God's Word

Read Genesis 2 and 3.

1. What are Eve's needs in the Garden of Eden?

2. How is Satan described in 3:1-2? What strategy does he use to cause Eve to doubt God's ability to meet her needs?

3. What are the results of Satan's deception for Eve? For Adam?

4. What is Satan's ultimate goal in tempting Eve to eat the forbidden fruit?

5. In Job 1:6-11 and Zechariah 3:1, we see Satan in action in the lives of Job and Joshua. Having read about his work in the lives of Eve, Job, and Joshua, what conclusions can you draw about Satan?

6. God doesn't leave Adam and Eve alone in their need. He comes to them and confronts them.

   a. What questions does God ask Adam and Eve?

   b. How do God's questions help Adam and Eve recognize that they are responsible for their actions?

   c. Why is recognizing that we are responsible for our addictions an important step toward recovery?

d. What provision does God make for Adam and Eve despite the fact that they have disobeyed Him?

7. Think about this passage. What lesson, encouragement, or hope does it offer you as you face bad things that look so good?

A Closer Look at Your Private Life

I use words like *glamorize, mysterious, magnetic,* and *glitter that attracts* to describe how Satan transforms something that is harmful into something that is compellingly beautiful.

1. How are you currently experiencing the kind of temptation that Eve did in the garden? What bad thing is Satan making look good to you? Be specific.

2. What might be the consequences if you chose to satisfy the desires you just identified?

3. Contemplate the scene where God seeks out Adam and Eve. How do you think they feel as God confronts them with their sin?

Do you think they recognize the confrontation as a sign of how much God loves them? Explain your answer.

4. Reflecting God's desire that we see things as they really are, the prophet Isaiah paints a vivid word picture of an idol stripped of its mystery and glamor. In the same chapter, Isaiah also writes about God. Read Isaiah 44 and then list some of the phrases Isaiah uses to describe God and the idol.

God (vv. 1-8, 21-23)   The idol (vv. 9-20)

Making What You've Learned Your Own

1. Nothing is more important than discovering and dealing with your hidden and secret addictions. While it's hard to recognize and admit our addictions to something bad, it can be just as difficult to see that our obsession with something good is really a hidden addiction as well. So close this part of your study by asking God to show you more of who He is and to give you the courage to see the object or event that controls you as He sees it.

2. God beautifully provided for Adam and Eve's needs by slaying an animal and clothing their nakedness. What hope does this give you?

3. Identify any attractions—bads that look good or an obsession with something good that has become an idol or addiction—that have gained mastery over an area of your life. Prayerfully consider sharing it with one other person who can begin now to pray for you in this area. If you haven't developed this kind of trust relationship with another person, I encourage you to ask God to help you find that special friend.

3
How Do Cravings
Get Out of Control?

How do normal appetites evolve into controlling dragons? What happens in the early stages of an addiction? Understanding the addictive process is an important step toward finding freedom from it. Seeing yourself through God's eyes is another step to freedom.

A Closer Look at *Fatal Attractions* (p. 34)

People who are addicted to food, sex, gambling, or anything else wonder how it happened to them. Actually, nobody understands exactly what causes people to become addicted. The problem would be easier to untangle if all the stories were the same. But since they aren't, it's hard to identify a single cause of the problem.

But that's not to say we have no idea concerning the process of addictions and how it happens. Indeed, the addictive process follows a well-worn path. By returning to the Garden of Eden we can see the emergence of a pattern. While Adam and Eve weren't addicted to the forbidden fruit, their story illustrates what happens to people in the early stages of an addiction.

1. On pages 35-39, the pages just following this excerpt, I outline four early stages in the process of addiction. What are those steps?

2. Why do you think justification is a core element of an addict's self-deception? And why do you think an addict doesn't recognize this faulty reasoning?

3. What is the alternative to denial? To blame?

4. Why do we human beings—addicts or not—opt for denial and blame over acknowledging the truth and taking responsibility for our own actions?

5. How does rationalization offer an addict protection? What are addicts able to avoid as long as they rationalize their behavior?

6. Why is isolation a natural next step in the addictive process?

A Closer Look at God's Word

Having looked at Satan's strategy of temptation and at the three stages of addiction, we will now look at the scene in the garden from Eve's point of view. Read Genesis 3 again.

1. Compare Genesis 2:16 and 3:3. How does Eve misquote God in 3:3? How do her words indicate that her reasoning isn't based on reality?

2. Look at verse 5. How does Satan cast doubts on God's integrity? What part of Satan's statement is true? What part is false? Why do you think Eve believes what Satan says?

3. Why do you think the idea of being like God appeals to Eve? What is wrong with her reasoning? (Remember that self-deception is a step toward addiction.)

4. Read again the conversation between God and Adam and Eve in verses 8-13. How does Adam fall into the blame game? What is he trying to do for himself by blaming Eve? What is Eve trying to do by pinning the blame on Satan?

5. On page 37 of *Fatal Attractions* I wrote:

> When we deny something, we refuse to admit
> it. When we rationalize something, we give good

reasons for our behavior instead of admitting the one true *reason*. Rationalization enables us to distract ourselves and others from the true nature of our problem.

We've seen Adam and Eve engage in self-deception, denial, and blame. Where in Genesis 3 do you see Adam and/ or Eve rationalizing their behavior?

6. Compare Genesis 2:25 with Genesis 3:7 and 3:23-24. How do these verses illustrate the isolation an addict experiences?

A Closer Look at Your Private Life

Where has this chapter been a mirror for you so far? Taking a good, hard look at yourself right now can be a critical step of understanding and an important move toward freedom from an addiction.

1. Self-Deception: Are you deceiving yourself about the degree of your involvement in a bad thing that looks good? Are you justifying your behavior?

2. Denial and Blame: Are you, like Adam and Eve, pointing the finger of blame at someone else? Are you denying the reality of your unhealthy, if not sinful, actions?

3. Rationalization: What good reasons are you telling yourself to explain your self-destructive actions?

4. Isolation: Are you, like Adam and Eve, isolating yourself from God and from people who are close to you in order to have the freedom to pursue your unhealthy actions?

5. Reread *Rituals* (pp. 39-40). Where do you see yourself in this section? Have you experienced the rush that prepares an addict for acting out? Put a check beside the statements you most identify with:

     _____ Sometimes I feel that living a good life is impossible.

     _____ I can never change. Sometimes I don't even want to.

     _____ Sometimes I wonder, "Can a person ever be truly right with God?"

6. What kind of person does God describe in the following verses?

     Psalm 51:17

     Ezekiel 36:26-27

     Luke 8:15

     2 Corinthians 3:3

     2 Timothy 2:22

Put a check beside the statement below that you would most like to identify with and write out a promise from

Scripture that supports the truth of the statement(s) you chose.

_____ I can be right before God.

_____ I don't have to keep on living a life of guilt and failure.

_____ I don't have to turn away from God.

7. Now reread *Loss of Control* and *Crash and Burn* (pp. 40-41). Does this description of surrendering to your dragon within frighten you? How do you react to the description of the shame which follows surrendering to the dragon?

Making What You've Learned Your Own

The close look at yourself which you just took is not meant to paralyze you. Instead, this mirror is intended to move you to action—action which will result in your freedom. As you start to take action, find comfort in this beautiful truth: "The reason healing begins with God is because He already knows the truth about you. He's not blown away by what you've said or done. He sees your flaws and loves you anyway. You're safe with God" (p. 42).

1. Write a paraphrase of Psalm 139:1-6. Simply put God's thoughts into your own words.

2. What phrase from the psalm touches you most deeply? Write it here and on an index card. Tape the card to your

bathroom mirror so that you can be reminded of God's love for you every morning as you start the day.

3. Ask God to give you the courage to lay before Him that area of your life you're most concerned about right now. Write it here if you feel free to do so.

4. Is there someone who can hold you accountable as you take steps toward freedom? Write his or her name here:

_____

Perhaps this person will even share a part of his or her life with you. If so, make a commitment to pray for each other.

4
Food—
Hungry for Love

It's hard to admit that we have an addiction of any kind. We're sure that, if people knew about our addiction, they wouldn't like us, and we are often convinced that God wouldn't love us either. And few people fear this kind of rejection like the compulsive overeater.

A Closer Look at *Fatal Attractions*

1. Finish this sentence which begins on page 46: Compulsive overeaters...

   a.

   b.

   c.

   d.

2. The first step a food addict needs to take is overcoming denial. This step isn't easy for anyone.

   a. Why is it hard to admit our weakness to ourselves? To others?

b. What do we fear?

c. How do you respond when someone shares with you his or her weaknesses, struggles, or sins?

d. How do you like to be received when you share your struggles?

e. Think about the people you know. Who may very well offer you acceptance if you risk being open about your struggles?

From *Fatal Attractions* (p. 47):

> For compulsive overeaters, the fear of rejection isn't the only reason they deny the seriousness of their problem. Food promises to fill their empty heart without any of the relational risks.
>
> • Food is always there in the crunch.
> • Food is always there to kill the pain.
> • Food is always there to give pleasure.

No wonder overeaters deny they're addicted. They have a lot to protect. Yet food will never satisfy the hunger in their heart. An empty heart can't be filled until an overeater stops denying the depth of his or her problem.

3. Do you have additional insights as to why food addicts sometimes go to great lengths to deny they have a problem? Be ready to share your ideas with others in your group.

4. In *Mirror, Mirror on the Wall* (pp. 48-49), I ask you to take an honest look at yourself.

- Do you look forward to events primarily because of the food that will be there?
- Do you constantly think about food?
- Do you eat when you're mad?
- Do you eat to comfort yourself during times of crisis and tension?
- Do you eat when you're bored?
- Do you lie to others about how much or when you eat?
- Do you stash away food for yourself?
- Are you ever ashamed about how much and what you eat?
- Are you embarrassed by your physical appearance?
- Are you 20 percent or more over your medically recommended weight?
- Have important people in your life expressed concern about your eating habits?
- Has your weight fluctuated by more than 10 pounds in the last six months?
- Do you sometimes think your eating is out of control?

5. Now that you have moved out of denial and acknowledged that you may be addicted to food, the next step toward freedom is understanding the addictive cycle. Your group will

probably want to discuss these further, but right now take some time to think about each step yourself. To do this, define each step in the space provided below and write out any insights you have about the addictive process.

Step 1: Preoccupation

Step 2: Ritualization

Step 3: Acting Out

Step 4: Shame

A Closer Look at God's Word

More than anything, food addicts need to have their faulty thinking replaced by the truth of God's love for them as revealed in Scripture. Just as parents' love teaches children that they are worthy and lovable, God's love enables addicts to know that they, too, are worthy and lovable. God wants you to know His love. He wants to be your Friend.

1. Read Ephesians 3:16-19 several times. What four things does God desire for you?

    a.

    b.

c.

d.

2. In the Bible, several writers describe Abraham's relationship to God as that of a friend (2 Chronicles 20:7; Isaiah 41:8; James 2:23). God also wants to be your friend, the kind of friend described in Proverbs 17:17 and 18:24. After reading these proverbs, write a thank you note to God. Thank Him for offering you the most perfect friendship you could ever want and ask Him to help you accept this offer and receive His love.

3. Four elements of an overeater's faulty thinking are:

- "I can fill my empty heart by filling my stomach with food."
- "I'm a bad, unworthy person."
- "No one would love me if they really knew me."
- "Food is my most important need."

In response to these wrong ideas, turn to the previous study and read your paraphrase of Psalm 139:1-6. Can you understand a little better now how valuable you are to God and how faulty the four thoughts above are?

A Closer Look at Your Private Life

Look again at the four elements of an overeater's faulty thinking listed in the previous question. Now rewrite them so that they reflect the truth of the Bible.

1. I can fill my empty heart...

2. I'm a...

3. God knows me and...

4. My most important need is...

Making What You've Learned Your Own

1. Personalize the point I make in *A Better Way* (p. 54) by writing, "My addictions can't be overcome until I..."

a. Identify your dragon: _____.

b. Write the name(s) of one or two people whom you can turn to for help.

2. Turning to God and other people for help may bring you to the point of evaluating some of the past pages of your life and letting yourself be loved.

a. What do you think is the source of your soul hunger?

b. Do you think it might be helpful to work with a friend or counselor?

c. Is there someone you can count on who is not afraid to put his or her arms around you and who accepts you but does not allow you to deny the truth of your addiction? Ask God to provide such a person or thank Him for the person He has already placed in your life.

5
Sex—
An American Obsession

Sex is one of the most wonderful gifts God has given us, yet its beauty quickly becomes tarnished when we become obsessed with sex. How does healthy sexual desire become a destructive compulsion? And, when it does, how can you find freedom from damaging sexual behavior?

A Closer Look at *Fatal Attractions*

1. Jot down one or two headlines from this week's newspapers that further illustrate the devastation of sexual addictions.

2. How can a church sometimes create an environment in which sexual addictions thrive?

3. Does the reluctance of Christians to discuss sexual issues contribute to the problem of sexual addictions? If so, how?

From *Fatal Attractions* (p. 59):

> What causes people to continue doing some-
> thing they know is wrong and has the power to
> destroy them? It's crucial to realize that sexual
> addiction is more than a problem with lust. For
> sex addicts, the compulsion to act out is so strong
> they're unable to resist the urge no matter how
> grave the consequences.

4. Jot down some of the consequences of sexual addiction,
either from the book or from your own observations.

How does the thought of experiencing some of these consequences make you feel?

A Closer Look at God's Word

Before we go further, let's look at sex from God's point of
view. What does He have to say about sex? Read Proverbs
5:15-19.

1. To what is a wife compared?

   a. (v. 15)

   b. (v. 18)

c. (v. 19)

2. In one sentence, state the main idea of Genesis 2:18 and Proverbs 18:22.

3. What conclusion have you come to about God's view of sex?

How can something good, designed by God, have such power to destroy? Working through the story of Samson's life will help you understand the devilish forces that are released when sex becomes an unhealthy compulsion. It will also help you better understand the addictive cycle.

As you read the story of Samson, you will see a powerful man, called by God to deliver his people, yet repeatedly acting out sexual weaknesses.

4. Read the words the angel of the Lord spoke to Samson's mother before he was even conceived (Judges 13:5-6). Write down a brief job description for Samson based on these verses.

5. Samson enjoyed God's blessing and the stir of His Spirit within. However, being chosen by God to do a great work didn't keep Samson from being vulnerable. Read chapters 14-16 for the whole story. Pay particular attention to the following verses: 14:1-2, 5-6, 12-14, 16-17; 15:1-6, 14-20; 16:1-31.

a. What do you discover about Samson's weaknesses in these verses? Include the Scripture references.

Example: 14:1-3—Samson demanded his needs be met.

b. What do you discover about Samson's strengths? Include references.

Samson's story illustrates what happens when sexual cravings get out of control, but God provides a way out of sexual temptation.

6. Read the story of Joseph and Potiphar's wife (Genesis 39:2-15) and 1 Corinthians 6:18.

a. How do these passages from Scripture fit together?

b. What can we learn from these passages?

c. How could Samson's story have been different?

A Closer Look at Your Private Life

1. It's again time to take a hard look at your own life. Do you see yourself doing any of the following? (See pages 61-62 for details about each step in the cycle.)

_____ Being preoccupied with sex

_____ Ritualizing your sexual actions

_____ Acting out your sexual fantasies

_____ Feeling ashamed for doing so afterwards

2. I've identified four common threads that seem to appear in every story of sexual addiction (pp. 62-65). Do any of these reflect how you think?

_____ I can regularly experience the exhilaration of young love.
Are you addicted to the adrenaline rush which comes with breaking the rules and obtaining the forbidden fruit?

_____ I'm a bad, unworthy person.
From your point of view, is your evil behavior perfectly consistent with your inherent badness?

_____ No one would love me if they really knew me.
Is the illusion of intimacy safer for you than building a relationship with a real person?

_____ Sex is my most important need.
Does sex give you a sense of being loved, accepted, and nurtured that you don't get in any healthy relationship?

3. List the levels of addiction and write a brief description of each (pp. 66-68).

4. Now *How to Know If You're Hooked* (pp. 68-69) will help you put all this together. Remember that you must be brutally honest as you answer these four questions. You can't deal with the dragon inside if you deny that he even exists.

- Is your behavior secret?
- Is your behavior abusive?
- Is your behavior used to deaden painful feelings?
- Is your behavior empty of genuine commitment and caring?

5. If you answered yes to one or more of the four questions above, look again at the levels of addiction. Do you see yourself somewhere in that list?

Making What You've Learned Your Own

In a later chapter, I'll talk more about specifics you can take to break the addictive cycle at its earliest stages. Right now, though, you need to know that God is for you. He's on your side, and He's throwing you a lifeline. Know, too, that He is the God of the first and the second and the third and the fourth chance. He will never give up on you.

1. Write out the following verses:

- Jeremiah 31:3
- 1 Corinthians 6:18a
- Hebrews 4:16

2. Now paraphrase those verses. Weave your name into the text so that you hear God talking specifically to you in these passages of Scripture.

6
Codependency—
Hooked on Helping

It's easy to look at someone who's a codependent and say, "There isn't anyone who's as giving as Paula. She never considers her own needs. All her energy is focused on helping others." But that kind of helping—also known as codependency—has some serious pitfalls and deep-seated causes. It isn't easy to leave behind a lifestyle of codependency— to let go of others and take responsibility for your own life— but you can do it.

A Closer Look at *Fatal Attractions*

1. Write out Melody Beattie's definition of a codependent (p. 71).

2. To help you understand how a person becomes a codependent, study the profile of a dysfunctional family (p. 72).

    a. Which role do you most identify with?

b. What dysfunction in your family forced you into one of the codependent roles listed on page 72?

c. Why was that role an easy fit for you?

Codependents often want to help people more than they want to be helped. Can you identify with my feelings when I explain how my payoff in helping troubled people was the emotional pleasure I derived from rescuing?

3. Think of a time you tried to help someone who wasn't ready to be rescued. Describe what you did.

4. What feelings and thoughts did you experience as you tried to rescue that person?

5. What consequences did you have to deal with as a result of attempting to rescue that person? What consequences did the person you were trying to help face?

From *Fatal Attractions* (p. 76):

My attempts at rescuing people who weren't ready to be rescued never helped anybody. On the contrary, it actually slowed their growth by protecting them from the consequences of their bad choices. God never relieves people of their responsibilities or the consequences of their actions. And neither should we.

6. Reread *Who's the Victim Anyway?* (p. 75).

a. Draw a triangle and affix to each point one of the three roles Dr. Kalpan says codependents function in (rescuer—persecutor—victim).

b. Think about a time when you tried to help a person (be the rescuer) but then found yourself getting angry with him or her (becoming the persecutor). How would you like to react that next time you find yourself persecuting someone who hasn't responded to your rescue?

c. How would you like to react when the person you are trying to rescue makes you the victim?

7. Reread *Destructive Actions* (pp. 76-79). Jot down specific details to help you understand how harmful these behaviors are.

Reacting:

Controlling:

Rescuing:

8. What emotions can alert you to your codependent tendencies when you are trying to help someone?

    a.

    b.

    c.

A Closer Look at God's Word

There are two specific steps you can take as you deal with your own codependency.

Step One: Let Go

Meditate on this thought: The best thing you can do for people who aren't ready to be helped is to let them go and trust God to take care of them. The father in the story of the Prodigal Son is an example of a man who lets go. Read Luke 15:11-32.

1. What do you learn about the father in this story—about his character, his station in life, and his relationships with his sons?

2. How does the father respond to the choice his son makes?

3. What do you think the father is feeling as his son walks away?

4. If you were that father, what would you have wanted to do?

5. What risk does the father take when he gives the son his inheritance?

What are the potential benefits of the father's actions?

6. What makes it difficult for you to let the people you love face the consequences of their behavior?

What makes it difficult for people in the church to let others face the consequences of their actions? (Review *Codependency in the Church* on page 76.)

7. What were your thoughts and feelings as you read about the Prodigal Son in the context of a discussion on codependency?

8. If codependent attempts to rescue other people have become habitual, practice the repertoire of options presented

on page 82. Which response feels most natural to you? How would you like to respond the next time you find yourself wanting to rescue someone?

Step Two: Find the New You

Our inaccurate sense of identity is what drives us to rescue people. God offers us a healthy and secure identity in His love.

9. You can begin to find the new you by meditating on 2 Corinthians 5:17. What does it mean to be a new creation in Christ?

10 What hope is there for you in the phrase, "The old has gone, the new has come"?

A Closer Look at Your Private Life

Spend time this week thinking about the role you had in your family while you were growing up. Look at your present relationships and see how you still function in that role. Try to understand how your old role is no longer serving you well and may even be hurting you.

Making What You've Learned Your Own

Is there a person whom you love who is right now making a choice that could be disastrous for him or her and for others? You've offered warnings about the consequences of that choice, but your words have not been heard... you've gotten angry... you've cried...

Find a quiet place and tell God the whole story. Share with Him your fears, your concern about that person, and how helpless you feel. Then acknowledge God's infinite wisdom and power and His deep love for that person. Ask Him to help you trust Him to care for that person.

You have now done the best thing you can do for the one you care about: you've released him or her into God's care.

7
Exercise—
The Natural High

Exercise is a good thing unless it becomes an addiction. What causes an exercise addiction? What are the dangers of such an addiction? And what can help free you from an exercise addiction *and* help you stay fit both physically and spiritually?

A Closer Look at *Fatal Attractions*

1. Make believe you are writing an advice column. Use information from *Fatal Attractions* to help each of the following writers.

> Dear (your name) , I started jogging a year ago. At first it was wonderful. And then it started becoming almost an obsession. If I don't run, I yell at the kids. I hate my wife. What shall I do? Just keep running?

> Dear (your name) , I want to start an exercise program, but after seeing what happened to my husband, I'm afraid. He's an exercise fanatic! Should I just sit around and keep getting fatter?

From *Fatal Attractions* (p. 88)

With so many positive benefits of physical exercise, you may wonder how it can become such a demanding dragon for some people. For exercise addicts, working out is more than something they do to stay in shape. *They have entered into a relationship with an experience that temporarily deadens their emotional pain and provides them with pleasure.* In order to perpetuate these perceived benefits, they will exercise harder and longer or seek more exciting experiences. Ironically, their craving for exercise often threatens their health and disrupts their relationships with family and friends. Yet when deprived of exercise they feel let down. The thought of cutting back seems absurd.

2. Are you addicted to exercise?

   - Do you exercise through pain rather than cut back and wait for your body to heal?

   - Do you find yourself exercising harder and harder in order to achieve the same pleasurable effects?

   - Do you experience depression, moodiness, and irritability when, because of injury or schedule conflicts, you stop your activity?

   - Do you find yourself looking for bigger challenges and greater risks in order to achieve the same rush you experienced when you first started your activity?

   - Do you find your mood altered during the course of your regular aerobic program?

- Have friends or family members expressed concern about the time you spend competing or working out?
- Have members of your family told you they think your sport or exercise routine is more important to you than they are?

A Closer Look at God's Word

We need to develop goals to help us live a life that is in balance. We need to be disciplined as we care for our physical health as well as our spiritual health. Attention to both these areas is vital for fitness.

1. Read 1 Timothy 4:7-10, in the Living Bible if possible. How do you think keeping spiritually fit acts as a tonic to the total person?

2. When Paul says that "physical training is of some value, but godliness has value for all things" (1 Timothy 4:8), he doesn't mean that we shouldn't take care of our bodies. Read 1 Corinthians 6:19-20. What does Paul compare our bodies to?

3. Describe what it means to you that your body is God's temple or dwelling place.

4. Being God's temple means that we're designed by God to show forth His glory. Prayerfully read the following Scriptures. Use them as guidelines to develop a set of goals that will nurture your inner spirit.

Psalm 1:1-2; 119:9-16

Psalm 5:1-3; Philippians 4:6

Psalm 95:1-7

Hebrews 10:25

A Closer Look at Your Private Life

Read Philippians 3:10-16.

1. How does Paul's goal to know Jesus, forget the past, and strain toward what is ahead correspond to the spiritual goals you wrote above?

2. Spend time meditating on this passage from Philippians. How can these verses help you make safe and sane goals for your exercise program?

3. Read Ecclesiastes 3:1-8. Rewrite 3:5b using words that will remind you to keep balanced in exercise.

4. If you are beginning to realize that you may be addicted to your exercise routine, what do you think is behind that addiction? What emotional pain are you trying to deaden? What shameful secrets or dark memories are you trying to avoid? Why do you need to exercise to feel good about yourself?

5. On page 93, I suggest three ways to break the exercise fix. List and define them below.

    Which is the best choice for you? Ask a trusted friend to help you take this important step toward freedom.

6. Write down one spiritual goal and one physical goal and share it with your friend. Ask that person to hold you accountable to working toward these goals.

    a.

    b.

Making What You've Learned Your Own

    Make it a goal to interrupt your regular exercise routine this week and take a walk with God. Use this time to slow down and sort through the issues in your life. Talk to God about each of those areas.

    In fact, take your walk now. Do it today!

8
Negativism—
Feeling Good by
Feeling Bad

What makes some people thrive on everything that's wrong with the world? How have these people been drawn into a whirlpool of pessimistic attitudes, thoughts, words, and behaviors? And why do they drag us with them? Understanding how someone can be hooked on pessimism and recognizing some of the causes of such negativism are important steps toward gaining freedom from a chronically bleak outlook.

A Closer Look at *Fatal Attractions* (p. 96)

> For "I can't" addicts, negativism is an orientation toward life. They look at life through a dark lens. Their outlook affects everyone they come in touch with. And the more intimate the relationship, the greater the pain.

1. Families of "I can't" addicts know well the pain of living with such a person. What do spouses and children of people hooked on negativism usually experience within the family? See page 97.

2. Reread *Getting High on Feeling Low* (pp. 97-99).

a. Explain the distinction experts make between *substance* and *process* addictions.

b. What are the short-term "benefits" people hooked on negativism experience?

1.

2.

3. List the six characteristics of a dysfunctional family which give rise to addictive negativism (pp. 100-104). Jot down helpful information about each one.

a.

b.

c.

d.

e.

f.

A Closer Look at God's Word

Negative people grow up feeling that they're never quite good enough. But God views us as deserving of love even though we're sinful. Learning to accept that love is part of growing up in truth.

1. Read 1 Corinthians 13:4-7. Rewrite the passage as though God Himself is speaking directly to you—as indeed He is! Write "My love" wherever the word "love" or "it" occurs and insert your name so that you can hear God speak to you through His Word.

"My love for you is patient, _____ .

My love for you is kind..."

2. Learning to speak the truth in love is part of growing up in Christ. Read Ephesians 4:14-16. How does speaking the truth in love help build a healthy family? How does it heal relationships?

3. Learning to get rid of anger, bitterness, and malice is part of growing up in Christ. Read Ephesians 4:25-32.

a. List the negatives and the positives alongside each other. Which qualities characterize your life? Which list do you want to characterize your life?

Negatives: *Positives:*

b. What hope do you find in these verses?

A Closer Look at Your Private Life

1. Is the dragon within the dragon of negativism? If you're not sure, take one or more of the following steps:

- Talk with a family member or friend. Ask him or her to help you see yourself as you appear to others.
- Listen to your self-talk for a few days. What are the tone and content of the words you say *to* yourself *about* yourself?
- Try to stop saying negative things. Work to let go of your negative attitudes and note how difficult it is for you to do so. What does this level of difficulty tell you about yourself?

2. If you've discovered that you're hooked on negativism, look closely at the following characteristics of a dysfunctional family. Which of the following characterized the home in which you grew up?

a. Love is conditional.

b. Taboo topics can never be discussed.

c. Root family problems are not successfully discussed, dealt with, and resolved.

d. Family secrets are guarded and passed on.

e. Feelings are denied, avoided, discounted, and suppressed.

f. Denial is normal.

3. Coming from a dysfunctional family doesn't excuse your wrong attitudes, but understanding the roots of your negativism can help you become free of it. In fact, now that you are an adult, you can counter the six principles listed above with statements of health and truth. For each of the six principles above which functioned in your family, write out for yourself a reason why you don't need to believe these negative lessons. Let Scripture strengthen your arguments for health. Don't hesitate to ask a trusted friend to walk with you through this process.

Making What You've Learned Your Own

A friend put Philippians 4:8 to work in a practical way when she recognized negativism beginning to stain her life. "Every day I wrote down the 'best spot' of my day in my journal. Writing them down even showed a little bit of what God is like. He wants me to enjoy my life and He's interested in the little things. Over a lifetime, little things count for a lot."

1. Write out Philippians 4:8 below. Spend several days this week meditating on this command. Then put the verse into

practice by recording "best spots." Do you see a pattern? Do these "best spots" tell you something about who God is? About who you are? About the source of a positive outlook and good feelings?

2. Get together with a friend and share your "best spots." You'll both enjoy it!

9
Workaholism—
Getting High on Success

Why do you work? People answer that question in a variety of ways:

- I work so that I can take care of my family.
- I work because I enjoy the challenges and the people I work with.
- I work because it's my life.

Choosing the last comment as your answer to the question, "Why do you work?" is one mark of workaholism, a potentially fatal addiction but one which you can indeed be free of.

A Closer Look at *Fatal Attractions* (p. 108)

Author and business consultant Diane Fassel calls workaholism "the cleanest of all the addictions." She observes that workaholism is socially promoted because it appears socially productive. People comfortably brag about being workaholics.

1. What's wrong with this kind of thinking?

2. Reread *Marks of a Workaholic* (pp. 109-110). List the six marks of a workaholic and any information that will help you discover how closely your own sense of identity is tied to your work.

    a.

    b.

    c.

    d.

    e.

    f.

3. Describe two patterns of workaholism (pp. 111-113).

A Closer Look at God's Word
From *Fatal Attractions* (p. 113):

> Overcoming your workaholism begins with a recognition that you have value apart from your performance. Repeatedly the Bible states that God loves us for who we are instead of what we do. You are the handiwork of your Creator, who shaped you while you were in your mother's womb (Psalm 139:13-16).

1. Read Psalm 139:13-16. How does it make you feel to know that God actually wove you into the intricate person you are? That before you were even born, He knew every day of your life and every hour of your day?

2. Turn to page 114. Slowly and thoughtfully read aloud the five reminders of who you are.

3. According to Ecclesiastes 5:18-20, what three gifts does God give us? (See pages 116-117.)

a. Which gift(s) do you enjoy regularly?

b. What would you say is the heart of Ecclesiastes as reflected and repeated in 2:24-25; 3:12-13, 22; 8:15; 9:7 and climaxed in 12:13?

   c. Finish this sentence: The greatest tragedy in life is the
_____ of missing _____. (See page 116.)

4. Read Colossians 3:17. How can this verse help you maintain a healthy attitude toward work? How can it help you balance work, family, church, and community responsibilities?

5. Write an account of an ordinary day. How would it be different if you took to heart the phrase, "It is the Lord Christ you are serving"? Think specifically about how that perspective might affect your attitude, your actions, and how you use the hours of the day.

6. Healing from workaholism requires acknowledging that we can't do everything in our own strength. It's only when we finally recognize this truth that God is free to begin a work in us. Read His invitation to you in Matthew 11:28-30. What thoughts and feelings do you have in response to His words?

A Closer Look at Your Private Life

1. According to the discussion on pages 113-115, what are two motivations for workaholism? Do you see yourself in either of these portraits?

2. Consider a typical week. Open your pocket calendar. What does your schedule—the way you spend your time—say about your values? Is your work more important to you than your family? Or is your family more important to you than your work—and is their importance reflected in how you spend your time?

3. No one will benefit more from meditation on God's Word than the workaholic. In his book, *Created to Worship*,[1] Norman Jewell explains what meditation is and how to do it:

> Meditation is consciously thinking through a single key principle or a phrase or two from a verse. You come at it from different angles. Personalize it through prayer.
>
> This morning I read Matthew 11:28-30 in my quiet time. All day my thoughts kept returning to Jesus' words, "I will give you rest."

Take these same verses in Matthew and spend an entire day meditating on them. Some of the questions Norman Jewell asked can help you personalize God's truth to your own life.

a. Since Jesus is inviting me to rest, what's keeping me from resting?

b. I'm tired. Am I exerting more effort than I should on concerns?

---

1. *Created to Worship* by Norman Jewell and Eva Gibson (Accent Books; David C. Cook Pub., 1991), pp. 83-84. Used by permission.

c. Why am I gripping my burdens so tightly, preoccupied with them instead of Him?

d. Jesus is inviting me to come and be yoked with Him. How can I experience this truth? What can I learn by being yoked with Him?

e. Don't stop with these questions. Ask others about the Scripture and yourself. Write down a prayer that personalizes what you're feeling and learning.

4. What perspective on work and rest did you gain from meditating on this short but powerful passage of Scripture?

Making What You've Learned Your Own

Joy is indeed a butterfly that flies away when you chase it. When you stand still, though, it lands on your shoulder. By slowing down and focusing on the simple things of life, you'll one day discover that joy has found you.

1. Look again at the Christmas tree of gifts God gives on page 117. What gifts can you add to that list?

2. Share your list with someone—and share the joy!

10
The Power of
Admitting You're Helpless

So you've recognized in yourself an addictive behavior? These next six lessons will help you develop a strategy to become free of that dragon. The first step involves recognizing your inability to find freedom by yourself.

A Closer Look at *Fatal Attractions* (p. 123)

> Even the most mature people struggle with their lower nature. For instance, few people love God more than the apostle Paul did. Yet Paul confessed, "I do not understand what I do. For what I want to do I do not do, but what I hate I do" (Romans 7:15).
>
> Paul experienced relentless warfare. He loved God and wanted to obey the laws of God. He longed for spiritual victory. But he found himself repeatedly doing things he despised. Instead of feeling free he felt enslaved to his sinful appetites.
>
> If you're hooked on food, sex, gambling, helping, or a host of other things, you know about

slavery. You know how it feels to obey the commands of a master who demands your submission.

1. With the help of a dictionary, write a definition for *freedom* and *slavery* and list synonyms. Also give a contemporary example of each.

    a. Freedom—

    b. Contemporary example of freedom:

    c. Slavery—

    d. Contemporary example of slavery:

2. Review *The Dragon Awakens* (pp. 123-124). Explain the difference between your core personality and your sinful propensity.

Which enables you to act freely? Which enslaves?

A Closer Look at God's Word

Read Romans 7:7-25.

1. Why were the Ten Commandments given to Israel?

    • verse 7

    • verse 12

    • verse 13

2. How does the dragon use the laws of God to gain dominion over our lives? (The section *Wet Paint—Do Not Touch!* on pages 124-125 may be helpful here.)

3. Count how many times the word *do* appears in verses 14-21: _____. Summarize Paul's dilemma as he described it in these verses.

4. Pick out contrasting phrases and words from Romans 7:6-25. Is this a real war or isn't it?

	The Law of God:	The Law of Sin:
v. 6		
v. 10		
v. 14		
vv. 22,23		
v. 25		

5. Have you experienced this war inside you this week? Describe your experience.

6. What one thing does the dragon want from you (v. 23)?

A Look Inside Your Private Life

1. When have you, like me with my BB gun, found your sin nature taking over?

2. When have you, like me with my alcohol and drug abuse, discovered a power within you that you couldn't control?

3. Paul expressed the essence of his conflict with sin in Romans 7:22-25. Write a personalized paraphrase of these verses. Make it descriptive of what you're feeling right now—and don't forget the last sentence! You're going into the dragon's lair in the next chapter and you need to know right now that there is hope.

Making What You've Learned Your Own

When we come under the dominion of our dragon, we are capable of doing anything evil—and, as you have probably realized by now, we are incapable of controlling that dragon on our own. You and I are helpless against our dragon, but that's a good place to be. Like Paul, David knew what it was like to be in a place of absolute helplessness. That's why he wrote Psalm 116.

1. What phrases from Psalm 116 speak directly to you? List them.

2. Thank God, the Dragonslayer, for the truths about Him you find in the psalm.

3. Meditate on these truths—on the comfort and hope they offer.

4. Share this psalm with a friend who knows about your dragon and ask him or her to pray for you.

11
The Freedom
of Living Without Shame

You've learned that admitting your helplessness to fight your dragon alone is the first step toward deliverance and freedom. Now you are ready to take the second step. You can enter the cave and break the dragon's power, exposing his shameful secrets to God's light.

A Closer Look at *Fatal Attractions* (p. 130)

> The dragon within is the reason you feel you're a bad, unworthy person. The dragon is the reason you don't believe anyone would love you if they really knew you. The fear that keeps you away from the cave is what causes you to keep others away. If they saw deep inside you they'd see the dragon. The people you value would think less of you. You could lose your chance for intimacy.

1. What does the part of the chapter preceding the paragraph above teach about the dragon—what he does, what he carries, and what he embodies?

2. Since it's hard to tell another person about your dragon, I encourage you to begin by telling God about it. Do so now. "Lord God, I have a dragon in my soul. It's..."

A Closer Look at God's Word

It is significant that God's first creative act on earth was to create light in a dark world (Genesis 1:3).

1. Imagine a world without light. Try to describe it.

2. How can darkness be a picture of life without God?

3. Read 2 Corinthians 4:6. In light of this verse, explain what the following statement means to you: "Darkness can't be altered or made better in itself. It can only be lost in the light."

4. What characteristics of light can you relate to God?

5. The disciple John was with Jesus from the beginning of the Lord's ministry. John went on to write five New Testament books: John, 1 John, 2 John, 3 John, and Revelation. Over and over in his writings, he gives us a picture of Jesus as Light.

a. Read John 1:3-9. How does John refer to Jesus and why is that description appropriate?

b. John understood that we can choose light over darkness, for God has power over darkness. In John 8:12, John records what Jesus said about Himself. He said,

"I am _____ _____ of _____

_____."

What does this statement mean to you?

c. What message of light and hope is God declaring through John in 1 John 1:5-7?

d. The apostle John emphasizes over and over that Jesus is light and power. Read the apostle's description of Jesus in Revelation 1:12-16 and fill in the blanks:

Jesus was dressed in _____. His eyes were

like _____, His feet like _____, and His

voice like _____. In His right hand was

_____. A _____ came from His

mouth. His face was like _____.

What does this image suggest to you about the One you call Lord?

e. John also emphasizes in this final book of the Bible how much God desires to be personally involved in our lives. Read Revelation 21:3-4. Write down the phrases that reveal Him as a personal God.

A Closer Look at Your Private Life

In the gospel John wrote, he often refers to himself as the disciple whom Jesus loved. He does it in this passage about the Last Supper: "One of the disciples whom Jesus loved, was reclining next to him" (John 13:23). Propped up on his elbow, his feet extended away from the table, John could lean his head back against Jesus' chest. There at that memorable dinner, he held a privileged place of nearness.

This privileged place of intimacy and nearness isn't just for John. It's for me. And it's for you, too. On page 133 of the text, I invite you to enter the dark cave with Jesus Christ, the Light of the World. If you haven't yet done it, I encourage you to do it now. There is power in the light of His presence and tenderness in His arms as He holds you close to His heart.

While you're there, I encourage you to write His words to you on an index card: "I see it all, and I love you. I see it all, and I accept you. All you've shown Me I carried away. It was nailed to a cross with Me."

On the other side of the card write: "God loves me and I accept His love. God loves me and I am His child."

Put the card in your pocket or purse so you can carry a reminder of His love and acceptance wherever you go. Let it remind you of your privileged place of nearness to Jesus.

Making What You've Learned Your Own

Since shame is at the core of addictive behavior, it's crucial for you to counteract your negative feelings about yourself

Doing so is a choice. You can choose to say, "God unconditionally loves me, and I receive His love and love myself." Naturally the dragon will fight this. It wants to cut you off from the only love that will satisfy. It wants you to wallow in shame, desperately seeking love in addictive behavior.

Choosing to believe that God loves you is choosing to walk with His Spirit. It is God's Spirit who helps us walk in His light. And being in His light means being able to know—in the fullest sense of the word—God and His unconditional and personal love.

Now do an acrostic on the word LIGHT. Choose a word or phrase which incorporates each of the five letters to help you remember who Jesus is and what He is like. (Example: "L" could remind you of Jesus' unconditional Love for you.)

L
I
G
H
T

12
Devoted to the
Dragonslayer

Have you ever noticed the law of human gravity operating in your life? This law says that a person gravitates toward the condition of lesser distress. In gaining freedom from the dragon, you can let this principle work for you once you recognize that the consequences of addiction ultimately cause far greater distress than the journey toward abstinence with all its benefits. Although traveling on that journey may not be easy, it is definitely possible when you say yes to God.

A Closer Look at *Fatal Attractions* (p. 138)

Since it's painful for any of us to stop an addiction, why would we be willing to undergo pain? Why would we give up the pleasure derived from the addiction?

First, we will want to quit when the physical and emotional pain of continuing our addictive behavior reaches disastrous proportions. Such things as hangovers, hallucinations, falls and bruises, and the loss of employment, family, and friends could make an alcoholic give up drinking. People with food, sex, helping, or gambling addictions all eventually experience their hellish consequences. When that happens, they want out.

Second, we may stop our addictive behavior when we see that the rewards of abstinence are greater than the pleasures of the addiction.

1. Take time now to think about and spell out for yourself some of the worst things that could happen as a result of your addiction and some of the benefits you could enjoy as a result of abstinence. The lists on pages 139 and 140 are reproduced here for your convenience.

    a. Consequences of My Addiction

        1. To my family...

        2. To my employment...

        3. To my health...

        4. To my reputation...

        5. To my self-image...

        6. To my finances...

        7. To my future...

    b. Benefits of My Abstinence

        1. To my family...

        2. To my employment...

        3. To my health...

        4. To my reputation...

        5. To my self-image...

        6. To my finances...

        7. To my future...

2. Now prayerfully consider your two lists and complete the following sentences:

The option I prefer for my life—addiction or abstinence—is...

I choose this option because...

A Closer Look at God's Word

Perhaps you've already chosen to stop your addictive behavior. Your choice involves turning away *from* those things that are destroying your life but it also means turning *to* something. To be free of your secret addiction, you must turn to God and give Him your life. God offers us forgiveness, acceptance, freedom from the dragon, a wonderful future, and the power needed for a victorious life.

Read Romans 12:1-2.

1. What is God asking us to do?

2. When we refuse to devote ourselves to God, what will shape our attitudes (v. 2)?

3. How is commitment to God like a marriage commitment?

4. Our willingness to grab hold of an idol in the form of an addiction reveals the hunger and thirst in our soul for something outside ourselves. When we choose an idol, we will not find nourishment or refreshment. The following outline of Isaiah 55 will help you think through the steps that you can take to satisfy your thirst for God. Find the verse or verses that go with each step.

     a. Realizing my need

     b. Recognizing the truth

     c. Responding now

     d. Repenting of my sin

     e. Resting in God

     f. Receiving new life, renewal

     g. Rejoicing in the assurance of God's love and care

A Closer Look at Your Private Life

On page 144, I encourage you to dedicate yourself to God. Reread that section now.

Writing a prayer like, "Lord, I choose to serve You rather than an addictive idol ..." will help you clarify what's happening inside your heart. But don't stop with one sentence. Pour out your heart to God. He loves you and wants to give you strength to help you stop your addictive behavior.

Making What You've Learned Your Own

1. We human beings make decisions based on emotions and decisions based on reason or logic.

a. In your own experience, which decisions have you been happier with—those you've made based on emotions or those based on reason?

b. Why do you think people tend to be more committed to decisions based on reason?

c. What is the basis for your decision to follow Christ?

2. Be on guard. Making a decision to devote yourself to God means the battle is on. The dragon will do everything he can to make you change your mind. Remember the conflict Paul described? Read Romans 7 and 8 and do a line drawing representing his struggle. Have one line represent the old life (beware, it's crooked and twisted); the other, the new life in Jesus. Be sure to show the triumph of the Spirit.

Your only hope in overcoming your dragon lies in your relationship with Jesus Christ. You, like Paul, can say, "Thanks be to God—through Jesus Christ my Lord" (Romans 7:25).

3. Ask your special friend to pray for you as the battle against the dragon rages.

13
Finding
the New You

It's hard to work through the feeling that you're morally flawed. It's hard to believe in God's love when you've long believed lies about yourself. But as we apply the truth of God's love to our life—to our thinking, our decisions, and our outlook—the dragon's power will be broken and we'll find the freedom God wants us to have. In fact, that freedom comes as you use in your life what you're learning in this study.

A Closer Look at *Fatal Attractions* (pp. 148-149)

Because shame is at the root of all addictions, it's crucial that you begin seeing yourself as God sees you. In chapter 11 I gave you some suggestions for learning to love and accept yourself. I'd like to take those suggestions a step further.

God's unconditional acceptance is often difficult to comprehend. You may wonder how He can overlook all the terrible things you've done.

Actually, He doesn't overlook them. On the contrary, Jesus died on a cross to pay for all the wrong things you've done.

1. When did you first learn that Jesus died on the cross to pay for all the wrong things you've done? (If this is a new concept for you, move on to the next section.)

2. What changes in your life occurred almost immediately once you accepted Jesus as your Lord and Savior?

3. To your frustration, what struggles didn't magically go away? (The next section will help you better understand the continuing existence of your dragon.)

A Closer Look at God's Word

1. Read Romans 4:5, 10:9-10 and Ephesians 2:8-9. Summarize the teaching of these passages in your own words.

2. An important concept to grasp is that when we trust Christ to be our Sin-bearer, we die—but our dragon doesn't. Romans 6 teaches that, despite the continued existence of the dragon, the new you has been released from the power of your sinful nature. Read Romans 6:1-23. Which words are repeated in those verses? List them and note how many times each one is used.

3. Look for the contrasts Paul sets up in the passage and write them down.

4. List the consequences of sin and the benefits of a life of righteousness.

5. For a moment, think about the passage as a whole.

a. Why do you think Paul personified sin as a master?

b. Do you think those people sitting under Paul's teaching might have been afraid that grace would lead to immorality? Why or why not?

c. What should a true understanding of grace lead you to do (vv. 15 and 18)?

d. Where will obedience lead you (vv. 15-16)?

e. What kind of person does God want you to become (v. 18)?

f. What benefit do you reap when you become God's slave (vv. 21-22)?

g. What is the eternal result of serving God (vv. 22-23)?

A Closer Look at Your Heart

The dragon has ways of whispering, "Since you're forgiven by God Himself, an occasional sin won't hurt you." Reread *Saying Yes to God and No to the Dragon* (pp. 153-154). Ask yourself these questions:

a. What do I need to guard against?

b. What is my responsibility?

c. How can I "give myself to God" and hand my body "over to Him for His purposes"? Be specific.

Making What You've Learned Your Own

1. On page 150, I write, "Paul teaches that all who believe in Christ are identified with Him in His death, burial, and resurrection. It's not that we lose our individuality. Instead, we are indwelt by Christ. Everything that is true of Christ is true of us." What hope for freedom does this fact give you?

2. If you are to find the new you who is free of addiction, you need to, by faith, believe that Christ has delivered you from sin and your addiction. Your union with Him is the source of your self-control.

a. Write out your own statement of faith that Jesus has delivered you from sin and will continue to deliver you from your addiction. Begin with, "Thank You, Jesus, for..."

b. How are you daily strengthening your union with Jesus?

3. On pages 154-155, I list three steps for victory that I encourage you to memorize. Writing out the three steps and the accompanying affirmations on an index card is a good first step. Also plan to work with a friend as you memorize these important statements. Being accountable to a friend will help you take a giant step toward victory over your dragon.

14
Breaking the Addictive Cycle

Finding freedom means more than avoiding the dragon's trap. It means reprogramming your mind. It means, for instance, developing the ability to identify and avoid dangerous situations. It means knowing God's truth and being able to call it to mind for strength when temptation strikes. The New Testament writer James gives you such truth in his letter.

A Closer Look at *Fatal Attractions* (p. 158)

It's important to realize that the dragon's emergence from the cave is part of a repeatable cycle. Earlier I noted the four stages of the addictive cycle: preoccupation, ritualization, acting out, and shame. I'd now like to look at these four stages from the perspective of James, the half-brother of Jesus, who wrote about the dangers of temptation.

It fascinates me that a man who wrote almost 2000 years ago so clearly defined the addictive cycle we struggle with today. The stages of temptation he mentions parallel the stages of the addictive cycle we've been discussing. James urged his readers to be aware of the process of temptation so they could avoid it.

1. What do you remember about the four stages of the addictive cycle? Refresh your memory by reviewing pages 49-51 of the text.

    a. Preoccupation

    b. Ritualization

    c. Acting Out

    d. Shame

A Closer Look at God's Word

Read James 1:13-15. Keep your Bible open to this passage as you carefully reread, with pencil in hand, pages 158-164 of *Fatal Attractions*.

1. *Preoccupation—Enticement.*

    a. How can memorizing large blocks of Scripture and meditating on God's Word help you disrupt the addictive cycle at its earliest stage, that of Preoccupation—Enticement? (See page 160.)

b. Choose a block of Scripture right now—perhaps one that's been especially helpful as you've progressed through this study. Write the references and the first verse below. You'll be given opportunity to share with your group the verses you chose and why you chose them. In the meantime, begin memorizing this passage.

2. *Ritualization—Conception.* Stop right now and write below, "After desire has conceived, it gives birth to sin" (v. 15). Underneath make a list of the rituals that lead up to your addictive behavior. Define what you must do to stop carrying out these rituals. Be specific. Be ruthless.

3. *Acting Out—Birth.* If we break the cycle at the enticement or conception stage, we won't act out our addiction. Read 2 Samuel 11:2-17; 12:11-14. Trace the addictive cycle in this account of David and Bathsheba by identifying the following steps:

Step 1. *Preoccupation—Enticement*

Step 2. *Ritualization—Conception*

Step 3. *Acting Out—Birth*

Step 4. *Shame—Death*

4. *Shame—Death*. Finish the sentence:

Addictive behavior always leads

_____. Explain why this is so.

5. God has something more for us than shame and death (James 1:16-17).

a. Where do the good gifts He wants us to have come from?

b. Who gives these good gifts?

c. What good gift does James describe in 3:17-18?

A Closer Look at Your Private Life

Another gift God wants to give you is a friend, someone who will walk beside you and help you cut off your addictions; someone who isn't afraid to look at the dragon inside your heart. Reread *Find a Friend* (p. 164).

1. Use the guidelines there to write a description of that special friend.

2. If you haven't yet found this kind of friend, bring your need to your Best Friend. Do it now. Ask God to bring you a friend who will be a source of strength and encouragement as you work to avoid the dragon's traps.

Making What You've Learned Your Own

God's comfort is like a warm blanket that He wraps around us when we're hurting and struggling. When we reach out and pull that blanket close around us, something wonderful happens. God enables us to take that same blanket He's wrapped us up in and offer it to a friend. You see, God's warm blanket of acceptance and love is big enough for our healing and for others' healing, too.

1. Read 2 Corinthians 1:3-4. Make it your own by changing the "us" to "me," the "we" to "I," and the "those" to a friend who is struggling in the same way you are.

2. Pray for that friend and then pick up the phone. Let him or her know what's happening in your life. Let that person know you care about what's happening in his or her life. You might even discover that this friend is part of the answer to your earlier prayer for a special friend.

15
Tools for
Tight Corners

In this final study, we're going to talk about keeping a tool box handy. However, the tool that's most important is your relationship with God. Nothing—and I mean nothing—can take the place of an intimate friendship with the great God of the universe. But first let's look inside the tool box together.

A Closer Look at *Fatal Attractions* (p. 168)

As you move forward with your life of freedom from addiction, you will face difficult tight corners. Temptations, disappointments, or relapses will cause you to fear you're not going to make it. At such times you'll feel like raising the white flag.

Don't do it! Instead, pull out a tool that will help you solve the problem and continue on. This chapter is a tool box filled with tools you can use when you're in a tight corner and to help you keep out of them. Read it carefully so you know where each tool is and how to use it. Mark those tools you may need first so you'll be able to get to them quickly.

1. List the 14 tools and explain briefly why each is important for the tight corners you will face.

2. Which one did you mark first? Why?

3. Since true intimacy is an addiction's greatest enemy, you'll want to reread *A Support Team* (pp. 169-170). What can a friend do for you that you can't do for yourself?

A Closer Look at God's Word

1. Reread the verses I keep in my tool box (pp. 175-177). Which ones do you think might be most helpful to you? Select one of the passages you listed and begin to memorize it today.

2. Scripture nurtures your relationship with Jesus Christ. Reread John 15:1-17.

   a. List the words that are most often repeated.

   b. How does the relationship between vine and branch illustrate the intimacy between a believer and Jesus Christ?

   c. List the vinedresser's responsibilities in the vine's production of fruit (vv. 1-10).

d. What is the purpose of the vinedresser's pruning (v. 8)?

e. What does it mean to live as a branch of the vine of Jesus Christ?

f. What is the key to our becoming all God wants us to be in our relationship with Him?

g. What is the result of remaining in Jesus? Note the four-part progression of fruit-bearing in verses 1-5:

_____   _____   _____   _____

h. Reread verses 7-12. Which verses in that passage refer to the following fruit?

   1. A life of prayer

   2. Obedience to God's Word

   3. Joy in the Lord

   4. Love for others

i. What are the greatest tests of genuine love (vv. 13-14)?

j. We are friends of Jesus if we do what He commands. What else indicates our friendship with Him? (See verse 15.)

A Closer Look at Your Private Life

God has chosen us to bear fruit, and He enables us to do so when He prunes us. The words translated *cuts off* (NIV) and *taketh away* (KJV) mean to lift up, bear, or carry.

In Jesus' day, the vinedresser gently lifted the vine's dirt-laden branches, tied the branches to the stake, and carefully washed away the clinging dirt. As the vinedresser repeated this process over and over, the vine experienced a gradual lifting up. The branch would be lifted, tied, lifted again, and retied, each time lifted a bit higher on the stake.

1. What does this image tell you about God's patience with you?

2. His forgiveness?

3. His tenderness?

4. What hope does this lesson from the vineyard put into your heart, especially for those times when you may fall and relapse into your addictive behavior?

Making What You've Learned Your Own

God longs to see fruitfulness in your life, and He will make you fruitful.

1. Personalize the truth of John 15:5b and Philippians 4:13. Substitute the word "Jesus" for "Him," and your own name

for "you" and "I." Know that these words of Scripture are for you.

2. Highlight what you've learned about the vine and the branches by drawing a picture of a vine complete with branches and fruit.

Jesus is the Vine. He is everything you need for life and godliness (2 Peter 1:3), a life of freedom from the dragon of addiction. May you sense His presence, rest in His unconditional love for you, and call on His power as you continue this journey toward freedom.

▼

Bill Perkins is an insightful and entertaining keynote speaker and seminar leader for corporate, institutional, public, and church audiences. He has addressed audiences across the United States and appeared on nationally broadcast television and radio programs. For further information on guest appearances in which he addresses such subjects as overcoming our secret addictions and cultivating personal and professional excellence, please call or write:

Bill Perkins
2331 Dellwood Drive
Lake Oswego, Oregon 97034

▲